Last Word's
Uncommon Women

Last Word's Uncommon Women

Edited by Celia Hayley

WEIDENFELD & NICOLSON

First published in Great Britain in 2024 by Weidenfeld & Nicolson
an imprint of The Orion Publishing Group Ltd
Carmelite House, 50 Victoria Embankment
London EC4Y 0DZ

An Hachette UK Company

10 9 8 7 6 5 4 3

By arrangement with the BBC
The BBC Radio 4 logo is a registered trade mark of the
British Broadcasting Corporation and is used under licence.
BBC Radio 4 logo © 2011

A CIP catalogue record for this book is
available from the British Library.

ISBN (Hardback) 9781474607643
ISBN (eBook) 9781474607650

Typeset by Input Data Services Ltd, Bridgwater, Somerset

Printed in Great Britain by Clays Ltd, Elcograf S.p.A.

www.weidenfeldandnicolson.co.uk
www.orionbooks.co.uk

Contents

Contents

Introduction

by Matthew Bannister

Let me start by dispelling a myth. None of the obituaries you hear on *Last Word* each week has been pre-prepared. Our colleagues in BBC News, who have to react instantly to the death of a famous person, do keep some obits on file. But each week, we start from scratch. On a Monday the producer sits down with a variety of different sources: the newspapers and the internet of course, but also information from BBC correspondents around the world, and nominations from the team and from listeners. The producer combs through the many people who have died that week, and compiles a shortlist of possible lives for coverage. This shortlist is then whittled down in discussions with the editor to four names, and the producer sets off to find the right guests to talk about them.

What are we looking for in our subjects? In a way, it's quite simple: the lives we cover need to have a good story at their heart. This yardstick leads to the chief joy of the series, which is that it is always a mixture: we want to tell you about people from as many different countries, spheres, careers and backgrounds as possible. So our programmes have featured scientists and singers, poets and politicians, campaigners, designers, mathematicians, judges, inventors, adventurers ... it's hard to think of a profession or activity we haven't covered. Most of all, it means that alongside the household names, there are also people who were not so famous or lauded in their lifetime. For instance, one programme featured the Pope – one of the most famous people in the world – but also Georgia Holt, a seven-times married singer, model, actress and stunt driver, who also happened to be Cher's mother. Her early story conjured a life lived on the edges of Hollywood during the golden age; her later years reflected the joy of her daughter's success in that same sphere. And I've never forgotten Flossie Lane, who was the landlady of a pub in the West Country. It was a tiny place, one of those very traditional spit-and-sawdust pubs, and she had run it with an iron fist for years. Jeremy Paxman had been one of her regulars, and according to both him and her other customers, she was well able to get the better of him in an argument. She was someone who had made a huge impression on her community, without being known outside it; the kind of fiercely proud and individual character that is perhaps vanishing from the modern landscape.

In the main these are the kinds of people celebrated in this book: those who may have been forgotten, or flown under the public radar, but whose lives were rich and colourful and full of the kind of detail that can conjure an entire era. For me, they represent some of the most rewarding moments of *Last Word*: discovering unsung heroes or heroines and introducing them to a wider audience for the first time.

Of all the thousands of people the programme has featured over the years, this book puts the spotlight on to the women, and in doing so it highlights an interesting cultural shift. By its very nature, an obituaries programme tends to be a backwards-facing mirror, reflecting society as it was thirty or even forty years before, when its subjects were at the apex of their careers. This meant that when *Last Word* started in 2006, it was sometimes a struggle to avoid the programme being dominated by men, because the generation that was dying out had had their heyday in the 1940s, '50s and '60s, when men held the positions of power in almost every sphere. Of course, women were making all sorts of contributions throughout that period, but they weren't so visible, and we had to work harder to uncover their stories. Nowadays I am glad to say that that has changed, and as a matter of routine we will pretty much always cover two men and two women each week.

The backwards-facing mirror also meant that in the early years of the programme, one of the main topics that always arose was how the subject's life had been affected by the Second World War – had they served, had they been displaced, had they suffered loss? The confluence of these two factors meant that in the early days, the women we covered had often been wartime spies, or served in the AAF, or more sadly had endured and survived the Holocaust:

we uncovered a huge number of stories of great bravery and often poignancy, sometimes hidden for whole subsequent lifetimes. (Nowadays, incidentally, the cultural landmark that we find ourselves negotiating is often the Swinging Sixties – were they the type to tune in, turn on, and drop out, or not? It's interesting in this book to see the story of Carolyn Cassady, who as a member of the Beat Generation bridged these two landmarks.)

Then there are the 'firsts' – pioneering women, like Sally Ride, the first American woman in space, or Anne Warburton, the first woman to be a British ambassador. Too often, these women's stories encompass the struggle they faced in breaking the glass ceiling. But it is heartening that – as you will see in this book – there is no shortage of women we cover not only because they were the 'first' to do something, but simply because what they did was so interesting. And even more heartening that as time goes by we are not having to dig so deeply to uncover them.

So we find great stories, and then our aim is to tell those stories as vividly as possible. And it is here that our medium – radio – comes into its own. Radio provides what no newspaper obituary can – the subject's voice. Anyone who has ever been bereaved will know how powerful a thing that is: perhaps the most evocative way there is of conjuring a person's character. The sound of a voice seems to penetrate right to someone's core, far more keenly than a photograph does. To hear a subject's own words speaking to us across the years is always an emotional experience.

Radio also allows us to use archive recordings – music and sounds – that add the context and texture to the era they lived in. Finally, of course, we interview people who were close to our subjects – often we will have one person from their professional lives, and one from their personal, so that we get the view not only from the lab bench but also from the Sunday lunch table. It is these encounters that really set the tone of the programme. Perhaps surprisingly there can be a lot of laughter, a little like those moments at a wake when people decompress from the formality of mourning. The loftier the subject, the more interesting it is to hear about their quirks and foibles, the small moments that somehow illuminate their whole personalities. From time to time, we do have tears as well. We are helping people to conjure up as vivid a picture of the person who has died as possible, and sometimes their emotions take them by surprise, because in telling an anecdote it almost feels as though the person is in the room, and their loss will suddenly hit them. But on the whole the mood is upbeat: because, above all, *Last Word* tells stories about life, not death. In each case we want to know how this person lived and what they achieved, conjuring them in their prime. It can be a huge challenge, compressing seventy or eighty years of a life into six or seven neat minutes of radio, but we have become adept at combining key anecdotes and incidents to give a rounded picture of character and achievements. The acid test is how often we get the participants coming back to us after the programme to say how well we captured their loved one's spirit.

All of which means that at the end of a recording I often find myself wishing that I had known these brilliant, engaging, extraordinary people while they were alive. And that is what I always want our listeners to experience too. The heroines – and sometimes anti-heroines – that you will encounter in this book represent only a fraction of the many stories we have told over the years, but they give a sense of the remarkable variety of human achievement we have celebrated. Each story is a window into the impact a single life can have, either on a large or smaller scale; taken together, they tell us something about our history and the changing society we live in. I hope, like the programme itself, meeting these women will leave you inspired, moved and uplifted as I have been by the privilege of telling their stories.

Women of Courage

In the treasure trove of stories that make up the *Last Word* recordings, bravery is a theme that crops up again and again: women who took the harder, more dangerous course to stand up for what they believed in, sometimes for a specific period, sometimes over their whole lifetime. The Second World War provides the backdrop for much of this heroism. As the generation of women that lived through the war reach the end of their lives, their obituaries recall a vanishing tribe: Holocaust survivors; resistance operatives; intelligence agents who faced down torture and survived. Often, their wartime experiences over, these women returned to peacetime lives without much fanfare, the medals kept in a drawer, the honours seldom referred to. But of course, these are the stories about the lucky ones: the ones that got to live on to old age. For every Eileen Nearne or Alix d'Unienville, there were countless others, unsung, whose lives were cut short years before their time.

Wartime heroism is only a fraction of the picture, of course. There are always women who have risked – and lost – their lives for causes they believed in: to bear witness to injustice; to fight for peace; to liberate their countries; or simply to help others. Some are featured on the programme precisely because their lives came to an end too soon, and a few of these accounts involve ongoing situations: the murders of Daphne Caruana Galizia and Islam Bibi are not fully resolved, and the ripples from such deaths continue to spread. But the value of *Last Word* is that it captures a moment. By talking to the people who knew the subjects best – and by using their own words – it takes the freshest impression of the person who has been lost. These interviews – poignant, shocking and brave in themselves – conjure these women's characters in all their humanity, at a point before their stories have been polished into legend.

Eileen Nearne

Born 15 March 1921; body found 2 September 2010, aged
eighty-nine

> *'They put me in a cold bath and tried to make me speak, but*
> *I stuck to the story.'*
>
> Eileen Nearne

When she trained as a wartime spy, Eileen Nearne was taught never to
reveal her secrets. She took the lesson seriously. Her story, one of heroism
and extraordinary courage, was only revealed when an MBE medal
and a stash of wartime French currency were discovered in her flat in
Torquay after her death.

Eileen was born in 1921 and brought up in Paris to an English
father and a Spanish mother. With the outbreak of war, the family
moved to London. Eileen, along with her brother Francis and older
sister Jacqueline, all enlisted with the Special Operations Executive
(SOE), the secret spy network set up by Churchill to help fight
behind enemy lines. After being dropped into France, Eileen was
caught by the Gestapo sending messages to Britain on a hidden
wireless. Her own words, from a debrief document dated 15 June
1945, describe what happened next in stark terms which nevertheless give a sense of the terror of these moments: 'I was arrested on
25 July 1944, at 11 o'clock in the morning. I had just sent a message
when through the window I saw the Gestapo arrive.' She managed,
just, to burn the message and hide the radio set, but it was not
enough: 'They searched the house and found the set. They also
found the one-time pad. They asked me questions about my code.

I told them lies.'

Professor Michael Foot, a former SAS man turned historian who wrote a book about the SOE, described for *Last Word* how she was taken to the Gestapo headquarters on Avenue Foch in Paris and interrogated about who she was working for: 'They said, "Come on, who are you working for?" And she said, "I have no idea who I am working for, I am just a little shop girl, I am doing this for fun!"' That was all that she said.' It was then that they used the cold bath, filling it with water and holding her in it naked and face-down 'until she all but drowned'. In the face of her continued refusal they did this four times, and then, 'as they got nothing out of her, they packed her off to Ravensbrück which was a sort of hell on earth.' She was to spend six months in this concentration camp.

In March 1945 she was sent from Ravensbrück into another camp in Silesia, a work camp. She herself described the experience with typical fortitude: 'I did not want to work in the factory and so they shaved my head and told me that if I did not work in twenty minutes I would be shot. I then decided to work.' But she also decided to run away, describing later how she and her companions managed, sleeping in bombed-out houses and in the woods, having a near miss with the SS, who asked for their papers and luckily were fobbed off with a story. In Leipzig a priest let them sleep in a church for three nights. The end came when they saw white flags and the arrival of the Americans. When she told them she was English, she was put in a camp.

But the experience of course left its mark. As Professor Foot puts it, 'Nobody who has been somewhere like Ravensbrück is ever quite the same again, and she was never quite the same again.' She worked for over thirty years as a nurse, thinking that 'she would try to do a little good to somebody'. She lived with her sister for some time before her sister emigrated to America, after which she lived alone.

She was an incredibly tough character. 'Tough beyond!' in Professor Foot's estimation. She could also 'talk the hind leg off a donkey – if she wanted to – but she preferred to remain silent'. He describes her beautiful manners, her ladylike voice. 'She was small, slight, unremarkable.' In his opinion, in her early life she was somewhat in the shadow of her taller, more glamorous sister, and this fed into her decision to join the SOE, because 'it might offer a possibility of her getting out of it, and doing something quite distinctive by herself. Which indeed she did because she trained as a wireless operator, which Jacqueline never was, and could thus play a different, and equally distinguished, part in the secret war.' There was, perhaps, a hint of sibling rivalry lurking.

It is probably impossible to quantify her achievement, but Professor Foot describes how she 'provided a lot of dropping zones for arms, for two railway sabotage circuits,' which 'imposed an important block on German attempts to send traffic by rail to the Normandy front'. She helped to bring this route to an end, 'a decisive part of the war, wholly unknown to the troops at the front. Till now.'

As for her motivation both in this effort in the intelligence, and in withstanding such violence, Professor Foot speculates that it lay deep in her character: 'Some degree of obstinacy was a great help to somebody who was caught by the Gestapo: "I am not going to answer that one, they are not going to get anything out of me!" She was very good at that! I think she might have made a very difficult wife, if she had ever married anybody.'

Albertina Sisulu

Born 21 October 1918; died 2 June 2011, aged ninety-two

Albertina Sisulu's life in many ways defined the long struggle against white rule in South Africa. She was the wife of Walter Sisulu, who spent almost three decades imprisoned alongside Nelson Mandela on Robben Island. During this time Albertina carried on the fight against apartheid. She was often persecuted for her efforts and yet continued to provide a refuge to the many ANC supporters who became part of her extended family.

Milton Nkosi, who headed the Africa Bureau of the BBC for many years, told Jane Little for *Last Word* how Albertina Sisulu was given the honour of a state funeral, and how its size and grandeur reflected the very struggle she had been involved in throughout her life: 'In many ways it got the rainbow nation together again. It got a lot of people throughout the country – even people who never met her – to come out and share their feelings, about what she stood for, her values, and her dignity in her fight against apartheid over the decades.'

Albertina's life was one marked by hardship and distinguished by quiet resilience. She was born in 1918, the same year as Nelson Mandela, and, like him, in the rural Transkei. She was educated by white missionaries and wanted to become a nun, but circumstances would lead to a very different calling, not least as a mother and grandmother. Her grandson, Moyikwa Sisulu, described her as an 'awesome grandmother', someone who brought him joy and support and was a 'pillar of strength'. While it was the more domestic, softer side of her that he bore witness to, just as in her more public roles she had at home 'all the integrity and all the humility that people speak of'.

Albertina's father died when she was very young, her mother was sickly and she had to drop out of school a number of times to look after her siblings; she had a hard childhood. Milton Nkosi described how this hardship proved to be a training ground for the resilience she would need throughout her life. At that early age, living in a small mud house and taking on the care of her siblings, '*there*, that's where her formative years of taking on huge responsibility began to form'.

In 1940 Albertina began work as a nurse at the Johannesburg Non-European Hospital. She worked alongside a girl called Barbie, who introduced her to her brother, Walter Sisulu, the man who was widely credited with recruiting Nelson Mandela to the African National Congress (ANC). So began a six-decade-long love affair, one that almost didn't happen because Albertina was so devoted to her younger siblings. When Walter proposed, her immediate answer was no, because, she explained to him, she had children to look after. He said to her, 'Do you mean you want to help them through their life?', and when she said yes, that was what she had been charged to do by her father, his answer was simple: 'OK – do you mind if we do that together?'

Albertina married Walter in 1944, with Nelson Mandela as his best man. She was warned that she was marrying a political movement, and so it proved. That year she was the only woman present at the founding of the ANC Youth League. She helped lead women in a mass demonstration against the hated passbooks which black South Africans had to carry. In the early 1960s, after the shootings at Sharpeville, the armed struggle was launched, and Walter went underground as leader of the ANC's military wing. She had to support the family and politically took on increasingly active roles. In 1983 she became a president of the United Democratic Front, one of the most important anti-apartheid organisations in South Africa.

But the greatest challenge was to come with Walter Sisulu's arrest and imprisonment. Milton Nkosi describes how, after Walter was sentenced to life on Robben Island, it was up to Albertina to take over as breadwinner for the family. Not only did she have to care for her own kids, but 'she also took on a lot of kids who came through politics, and others just came through social work, really, because even though she was a nurse, she was also, in many ways, a social worker'. It was in her nature to help people with their issues. Throughout all this, she was under constant political pressure herself. She spent seven months in solitary confinement, was arrested multiple times, and at one point was charged with treason. This was standard for politically active people at the time. 'A lot of political activists were locked up, banished, for many weeks, and many months,' says Milton Nkosi. Albertina's situation was particularly bad because 'her husband was already in prison, and she had children at home. But she was constantly raided by the apartheid police, particularly a wing within the police called the Special Branch: they would pay her visits, each time she turned up for a meeting, they would use that as an excuse to lock her up as a threat to national security.'

In 1989, Albertina was finally allowed a passport. She travelled abroad and met George Bush Senior, and Margaret Thatcher. Later that year Walter was released. The description by Milton Nkosi of their reunion is a wonderful evocation of a personal love story, but also of an era of hope and change in their nation: 'He turns up in Orlando West, and they look like they had just met, they looked like they were sweet sixteens. I was standing outside their house at the time, and it was a remarkable thing to see, this elderly dignified couple not just being political leaders, but also being so ordinary in their love for each other.' It was a sight that 'really lifted the spirits of the people who were standing with us – the thousands who were singing outside their house in October of 1989 ... when they got together again it felt like sort of the end of a Hollywood movie. And there was a moment when they had a bit of a whisper to each other and Albertina just lay her head on Walter's shoulder, and she looked like a sixteen-year-old girl.'

After Albertina's death, she was referred to as 'the mother of the nation', not least by the ANC treasurer general. Since this was a title often given to Winnie Mandela, the honour caused a certain amount of concern: 'Of course, the whole country thought: "Oh my goodness, what is that going to do to Winnie?" Because she is generally known as the mother of the nation,' Milton Nkosi said. 'But actually, Winnie came to the night vigil, the night before Albertina's funeral, in Soweto at the Holycross Church, in Orlando West, and said that Albertina Sisulu is the mother of the nation.'

Walter Sisulu, her husband of fifty-nine years, predeceased Albertina in 2003; she was survived by her large family of children and grandchildren.

Lakshmi Sahgal

Born 24 October 1914; died 23 July 2012, aged ninety-seven

Lakshmi Sahgal was an Indian doctor and social campaigner who raised a regiment of women to fight against the British during the Second World War. She went on to join the Communist Party, to become a member of the upper house of the Indian parliament, and to stand for the presidency.

For Mark Tully, the BBC's former correspondent in Delhi, she was 'a doctor for the poor, a doctor with tremendous social conscience.' He found her 'very happy to talk about herself and very, very, happy to talk about her views on the need for social reform in India'.

Lakshmi Sahgal's daughter, Subhashini Ali, gave a more personal view, describing her simply as, 'very magical . . . You couldn't be in her company for five minutes without falling in love with her, and you never fell out of love with her,' although the social activist side of her personality was never far from the surface: 'nothing could really shake her in her commitment' to the causes she cared about.

This was evident from an early age; Mark Tully describes her as having a social conscience since she was a child: 'There is a story told about her as a child that one day she deliberately went out and got hold of a tribal girl and held her by the hand and brought her home to play, much to the horror of her grandmother, who believed that even if a shadow of tribal, or untouchable, girl passed over her she had been polluted.'

According to Mark, Lakshmi first became involved with the Indian National Army and its fight against the British in Singapore after going there as a doctor for the immigrant Indian community. It was there that she met the leader of the Indian National Army,

Netaji Subhas Chandra Bose. It was his idea to have a women's reg-iment, according to Subhashini Ali, 'because women will fight most hard for independence, and they need it the most'. This, as Mark Tully emphasises, was at that time 'a totally revolutionary idea', and one that many people doubted she could achieve.

But she did. In fact, says Subhashini, even she was surprised by the level of response she got: women who were willing to volunteer because they felt so strongly about independence. The aim of the Indian National Army was to help the Japanese defeat the British in India. Lakshmi's regiment, the Rani of Jhansi, was present in the Burma campaign, one that was particularly brutal. To Lakshmi's disappointment, though, says Mark Tully, the women's regiment was never allowed to do what she had trained them for, which was to fight.

She was arrested by the British in 1945 and held under house arrest for about a year. According to Subhashini, she made the most of this time. Being very beautiful and from a privileged family, she knew quite a few of the Indian Army officers who were friends of the family. So she managed to have 'a good time' in spite of her arrest.

But her military efforts were only part of her story, says Mark Tully: 'Her work as a doctor – that's what really made her reputation.' In later years she became politically active, becoming a commun-ist in the 1970s and later being given a seat in the upper house of Parliament. Eventually, 'a group of leftist parties also put her up as candidate for the president of India. She put up a good fight, but she was never really going to beat the main political parties.'

To grow up with Captain Sahgal as a mother was a very particu-lar experience, according to Subhashini, and not something that she always appreciated when she was a child. The young Subhashini would complain that her mother always had time to worry about other people's health, and not that of her own children. Her answer? 'Well, don't worry, you will be all right, you will always have enough people to look after you, but what about the people who don't have anyone to look after them?'

She was driven by a strong conviction that society needed to change. It was as though she simply could not understand how anyone could tolerate the huge social inequities that existed in India, says Mark Tully. 'You know, every day, as a deliberate act, she used to sweep the pavement outside her little clinic to demonstrate to everyone that she wasn't bound by any caste rules or anything like that, she wasn't ashamed to do what in the caste system is regarded as one of the lowest of the low jobs.'

It was a principle she carried with her throughout the whole of her long life.

Lieutenant Islam Bibi

Born 1976; died 4 July 2013, aged thirty-seven

Lieutenant Islam Bibi was one of the few senior women in the Afghan police force. She was shot, aged thirty-seven, while riding on a motorbike with her son-in-law in her home town of Lashkar Gāh in Helmand Province, and she died later in hospital. A month beforehand, in June 2013, Afghan forces had taken over responsibility for security in the country as NATO prepared to depart. At the time this episode of Last Word *was recorded, it was not known who carried out the attack.*

Matthew Bannister spoke to the *Daily Telegraph*'s former Afghan correspondent, Ben Farmer, who had interviewed Lieutenant Bibi earlier in 2013. He described his first impressions: 'She was dressed in her uniform, which is a drab olive-green uniform with a head-scarf, but she had a big smile.' He met both her and her deputy and was struck by the friendliness of their relationship, the jokes they made and the openness of Lieutenant Bibi herself: 'Often, as a journalist, trying to get these women to talk is very difficult, but she couldn't wait to tell her story.'

She gave two reasons for having joined the police force. The first was financial, as her husband's job as a hospital porter wasn't enough to support the family. 'I think they had either five, or six, children, and they struggled.' But as well as that, she was 'quite idealistic about it'. She thought this was the perfect way 'to do something for Afghanistan, the country she loved'. She was proud of the uniform she was wearing. '"Proud" was a word she used several times. She had seen the Taliban and she hadn't liked what she had seen at all and she wanted to try and "advance her country", as she put it.'

The reaction from her family when they were told she wanted to join the police force was 'very difficult', says Ben Farmer. Her family, and especially her brothers, were violently disapproving. 'One brother in particular threatened to kill her on three separate occasions,' going so far as coming to her house armed to forbid her to join. 'In the end the police had to come and take away his pistol.'

It shows great strength of character on her part that she was able to withstand that kind of pressure. Ben's estimation of her was of 'a very strong woman ... a strong character. She cracked jokes, she was very friendly, she was very open.' But underneath all that was a strain: 'The constant opposition within her family was quite wearing and it was something that had not gone away.' To add a further layer of complication, Islam suspected that some of her relations were Taliban sympathisers, so her position as part of the government forces put her in 'deadly opposition'. By the time Ben met her, the arguments within her family about her joining the force had been going on for over eight years.

But she was aware of the risks she was taking: 'Being a police officer, whoever you are in Helmand, is a very, very, tough job,' says Ben Farmer, 'They take really terrifying levels of casualties.' And the proportion of women officers is tiny: 'I think less than 1 per cent'. These women officers endure 'a lot of harassment, even a lot of abuse, and they are not well looked after. They are treated as second-class officers'. This extends even to simple things such as the lack of women's toilets at the stations.

Was Lieutenant Bibi conscious that she was in a way a role model, somebody who was blazing a trail for other women in Afghanistan? 'I think so,' says Ben Farmer. 'One of the most touching things she said to me was that she wanted her daughter to follow in her footsteps.'

Postscript:

It is still not known who killed Lieutenant Islam Bibi, and her murderers have not been brought to justice.

A month after Lieutenant Bibi's assassination, her deputy and successor as Afghanistan's highest-ranking female police officer, Lieutenant Negar, was shot in the neck and killed while walking near police headquarters. Once again, no group stepped forward to claim responsibility for her death.

Alix d'Unienville

Born 8 May 1918; died 10 November 2015, aged ninety-seven

Alix d'Unienville was one of a small group of women who joined the Special Operations Executive during the war and were involved in highly dangerous undercover work behind enemy lines. She was born to a wealthy French family living on the island of Mauritius. They moved back to France when Alix was six years old, and she was brought up in a château in Brittany. This came to an end when, after the German invasion, the family fled to Britain and Alix began working at General de Gaulle's Free French Headquarters in London.

The SOE historian Marcus Binney spoke to Matthew Bannister for *Last Word*, and described how one day Alix d'Unienville was ordered to report to the secret offices of the British SOE. As she set off, she realised that she had forgotten the address. 'She went to see a group of taxi drivers and said: "There is a hush-hush headquarters I need to get to," and they said: "Oh yes, we all know *that*," and it was a great joke that all the taxi drivers in London knew where SOE's headquarters were. So they bundled her in the taxi and she arrived on time and unflustered.'

Alix herself described in her own writings her early days in the SOE – she started out as one of the only two French people there, and almost immediately the other one broke his leg and left, leaving her as the only French person and the only woman. There were two Belgians, a 'terrifying pair', but they held her in 'utter contempt', she said: 'They were real professionals, real killers who had been in commando operations. The stories of their gun fights set my heart racing.'

In Marcus Binney's account, her most vivid memory of the

accelerated training she went through was of the parachute jumps. These were not high – about 400 or 500 metres – and the women would go first to encourage the men. Her own writing gives a vivid sense of what it felt like: 'In thinking of it, after all these years, I still feel the blood beating in my ears while crying: "No! No!" ...At the moment of the jump there is a sense of absolute emptiness and the shock of the parachute opening brought me back to consciousness. I felt an unexpected joy, a peace, a miraculous silence.'

Her mission in France, according to Marcus Binney, was 'to deliver this enormous amount of money'. This was split between a bag of 2 million francs which was tied round her waist like a cushion, but she also, 'to her horror, had to carry a suitcase with 40 million francs in it'. Further missions included couriering messages back and forth in the run-up to D-Day.

All of this was done under the fear of being captured, and indeed, says Marcus Binney, 'She was arrested. They quickly found her cyanide pill and they knew these particular cyanide pills were only issued to agents in London, but fortunately, in all the hustle and worry about everything, they forgot about that.' In fact, she had other incriminating evidence on her at the time, including a metro ticket. As they arrested her she 'suddenly remembered that she had written on the back of it the name of a contact. And of course that was the one thing that you were trained not to do.' She asked repeatedly to be allowed to go to the loo, and when they finally agreed she took the opportunity to dispose of it by eating it. 'Just as she swallowed it, he burst in to see what she was doing.' She got away with it, but it must have been a heart-stopping moment.

They took her to Fresnes prison, says Marcus Binney. 'Her mind immediately was on escape ... She decided to feign that she was going mad, and she was such a good actress she actually convinced them. But the Germans put them all on trains.' Her opportunity came when the train stopped due to the line ahead being destroyed by bombs. The prisoners were taken off the train and forced to march instead. 'She thought: "This is my moment," and she slipped out of the column and found herself by a doorway and she turned the handle and it opened.' She was inside a house, looking at a

French family. 'They were amazed to see her, but the man put his finger to his mouth and said: "Be quiet," and she had to sort of crawl across the floor. They took her quietly upstairs and said: "You must not go near the window."' She stayed there for about half an hour, and then ran across the fields. From that point, 'she was passed from one family to another. Not so much later she was back in Paris being driven back in an American jeep.' The escape saved her life, he believes: otherwise she would have died at Ravensbrück, where so many other women perished.

It was later in her life that she met Marcus, who described her as 'very sweet and self-possessed, very cool and determined'. She was awarded the Croix de Guerre and the Légion d'Honneur and a military MBE in the UK. She was proud of her achievements, 'but in a modest way. What she said wistfully was that "The one medal I wanted was the medal for escapers and that's the one I didn't get!"'

Her own writings give an impression of the almost dreamlike but nonetheless terribly real danger of those days: 'Many of my comrades were arrested, many are dead. Of others I know nothing, and I never will know anything, because I have forgotten their names. Only here and there floats a young face, a gesture, a word, a smile, an anecdote. All the rest has plunged into the shadows.'

Salome Karwah

Born 1988; died 21 February 2017, aged twenty-eight

Salome Karwah was an Ebola survivor who went back to her native Liberia to help others suffering from the highly contagious virus. She died at the age of twenty-eight from complications that arose in childbirth.

Salome Karwah's father was a community doctor in the Liberian capital, Monrovia, while Salome and her sister Josephine were nursing assistants. Liberia was at the centre of the Ebola outbreak and when the disease arrived in the country in 2014, the family were among the first to be infected. Salome's father and mother died, and her sister lost her unborn child. But Josephine, Salome and her boyfriend and, later, husband, James Harris, survived.

In 2014, *Time* magazine made Salome its Co-Person of the Year, alongside several other Ebola fighters. Aryn Baker is Africa editor of *Time* magazine, and she described Salome as 'one of the most extreme cases' of Ebola. As she grew familiar with the disease from covering the outbreak, Aryn came to recognise that 'there were signs that you know someone is not going to make it. Very bad hiccups are one of them and she had the hiccups.' Salome knew well from all her nursing experience and seeing people suffer from Ebola that this was a fatal sign. So even to Salome herself 'it was a miracle that she survived'.

It was never entirely clear whether being a survivor gave her immunity from the disease, though it was commonly believed that you would be immune for at least a few years. Aryn says Salome used to joke about that, saying, 'This is my superpower, I have lived through it, I have survived, so now I am immune.' She put that superpower to good use when she heard that Médecins Sans Frontières was looking for survivors to volunteer at their clinic, 'the very one where she had been treated'. They were looking for people who could support the patients, but it was a role that would require a great deal of courage, a quality that she had in abundance: 'Not only courage, but a sense of doing what is right. Because, in her community, it was bad enough that she had survived the disease but also that she was going back and working with more Ebola patients. Her community didn't understand it, they shunned her.'

Around the Ebola treatment facility were two quarantine rings that kept health workers apart from their contagious patients. But Salome went straight through to the centre to offer hands-on help to the Ebola sufferers. 'She was able to bathe small children that were completely feverish; she was able to feed old men who couldn't feed themselves.' Aryn describes seeing the effect she had on patients who had been starved of all human touch for up to two months: 'Seeing her being able to cradle a child in her arms just made me realise: that's the story I want to tell, of a woman who can actually touch when nobody else can.'

Her own death three years after the outbreak was tragically avoidable, says Aryn. 'One of the most dangerous patients that a doctor can treat in the time of Ebola is a woman about to give birth, because there is blood; and blood is the most easy carrier of the Ebola virus.' This meant that when Salome went into hospital to have her baby; even though people might rationally know that an Ebola survivor was not going to transmit it any more, 'the fear is still there'. She successfully underwent a caesarean section and delivered a healthy baby. 'But within a few hours of getting home she started convulsing, and James and her sister tried to take her back to the hospital. The nurse practitioner and the doctors on staff saw the convulsions – they had flashbacks, probably, back to Ebola time because convulsions were another sign of Ebola – and they refused to treat her. It was a combination of bad maternal care to begin with and the fear of Ebola that ultimately resulted in her death in the hospital that day.'

She was twenty-eight years old when she died, a wife and

mother of young children. Aryn Baker's final description is simple, but devastatingly sad: she was 'somebody who had saved so many lives, and not just saved them. For the people who did die, at least in their final moments they had someone holding them, feeding them, caring for them and telling them that they were going to be OK.'

Salome was survived by her husband and her four children, including the newborn baby, Jeremiah.

Jeannie Rousseau

Born 1 April 1919; died 23 August 2017, aged ninety-eight

Jeannie Rousseau was a French intelligence agent who risked her life many times to smuggle secrets from German officers to the British during the Second World War. She had a photographic memory and was able to alert Churchill's government to the development of V-1 flying bombs and V-2 rockets.

Jeannie was the daughter of a formidable civil servant who didn't feel she was worth speaking to until she was thirteen years old. Her wartime role wasn't publicly revealed until she was in her seventies, when she gave an interview to the journalist David Ignatius. He spoke to Matthew Bannister for *Last Word*, describing how the family had moved to Brittany after the German invasion, and it was there that Jeannie began her undercover work, based first of all on the fact that she was a skilled linguist. Her almost fluent German meant that she could pass for a German herself to the occupying soldiers. 'So she began passing secrets that she would pick up in conversation with German officers she'd talk to.' The dramatic increase in the number of attacks on Germans in this particular area led them to suspect that there was some kind of leak. 'They began rounding up people, and Jeannie was arrested in those early days – she was then a girl perhaps of twenty – and was taken to the prison at Rennes. She was never broken and didn't confess; she was released on condition that she would leave the coastal area that was so sensitive and [she] went to Paris.'

Jeannie's family friend, Jeremy Orme, picked up the story, describing how 'a chance encounter with one of her previous teachers led her to form a connection with one of the subsets of the biggest resistance intelligence-gathering organisations Alliance and the subset Les Druides.' She joined this organisation under the code name Amniarix, and it was in this way that she provided information which came through to London. When Jeremy once asked her whether her network supplied information to de Gaulle's Free French or to the British, 'the *immediate* reply, with a degree of vehemence was ... "to the *British*, of course". Which I took to be not so much anti-de Gaulle but a cool-headed assessment: where would the intelligence eventually be most useful?'

As David Ignatius described it, 'She had befriended German officers who loved to talk with this charming, really quite beautiful, young French woman.' They were remarkably free with their conversation: they would 'talk about their exploits, talk about their secrets and, hard as it is to imagine, some of these officers began to talk about a programme that was under way in eastern Germany at a place called Peenemünde, where the Germans were developing extraordinary new weapons that would change the face of the war.'

These extraordinary weapons were in fact the V-1 and V-2 rockets. 'Her most important information related to the research and production programme for the flying bombs, the V-1 and the V-2,' says Jeremy Orme, explaining that the information she provided found its way to the attention of a scientific intelligence analyst, Reg Jones. Jones was reporting 'almost directly, I believe, to Churchill'. And it was as a result of this and other intelligence that the RAF was sent to bomb the production facilities. This 'seriously degraded the German ability to get this programme up and running'.

The intelligence provided by Jeannie was so impressive that an order was made that she should be transferred. The plan was that she would be 'brought by night secretly across the Channel by boat, to be debriefed in London. Somewhere there was a betrayal, but the Germans who had captured them did not know who she was or what was going on.' Nevertheless, she was imprisoned.

After this capture, David Ignatius says, 'Jeannie was sent to three different camps. In the first, she, with other women prisoners – other incredibly courageous French women – rebelled and refused to make the ammunition that they were being ordered to make.' By a stroke of good luck, when the Swedish Red Cross came to the camp she was one of the names on their list. 'They called out her name. The guards in this camp prevented Jeannie from answering, but, incredibly, as a prisoner, half dead, she managed to intimidate her German guard. She was released and taken by the Swedish Red Cross.' But he also points out that all of this must have weighed hard on Jeannie: 'I think there must be, for someone who lived through that kind of hell on earth, a sense: "How did I survive when so many around me didn't?"'

After the war Jeannie became one of the top interpreters at the United Nations. She married and had children, and in later years was presented with awards for her wartime work including the Légion d'Honneur, the Croix de Guerre, and the CIA's Agency Seal Medal. She was a regular visitor to Jeremy Orme's home in London and he describes a visit they made together to the Imperial War Museum: 'She froze just before the top of the steps on the way up. She didn't move. And after a little while I said: "Jeannie: are you feeling all right? Is there some problem?" And she says to me: "I'm quite all right", and she pointed up high at the top of the atrium.' She was pointing at the V-1 and V-2 bombs that the museum has hanging there. 'She was looking at them, and she said: "I never understood that that was their comparative size. I had seen engineering drawings, I had heard about them, I had never understood that one of them is so big, and the other one comparatively small."'

His last words on his friend speak to the core of the kind of person she was: 'I had exchanged notes with her at some point about a poem by Gerard Manley Hopkins in relation to Henry Purcell. It says, and begins, with the words:

Have fair fallen, O fair, fair have fallen, so dear
To me, so arch-especial a spirit as heaves in Henry Purcell

Her interest in that, and what that says itself, is all that one needs to know about Jeannie.'

Daphne Caruana Galizia

Born 26 August 1964; died 16 October 2017, aged fifty-three

'The weather was fine, typical for October in Malta,' says Mario Xuereb. He was in the newsroom of his employer, Malta's Public Broadcasting Service, when a tip-off came in about a possible car bomb. His first re-action was telling: 'We asked ourselves: could it be Daphne?' Tragically, it was: Daphne Caruana Galizia died when a bomb blasted through her car.

Daphne was known for her outspoken campaigns against corruption in Maltese public life. Working first for the *Times of Malta*, and then through her own much-read online blog, she was not afraid to name names and make enemies. Most recently she had used information from the Panama Papers – the leaked documents that exposed the activities of international offshore entities – to target leading figures in the island's political establishment. For *Last Word*, Matthew Bannister spoke to her sister Corinne Vella in the immediate wake of her murder, at a time when the country was in shock and Daphne's death was making headline news around the world.

Daphne was born into a middle-class family and educated at one of Malta's leading girls' schools, St Dorothy's Convent. Her sister's description of their upbringing was one of an open-minded and intellectually curious household: 'We grew up with the idea that the world was a much bigger place than we actually lived in ... and there were all different kinds of people. Books, magazines, newspapers, ideas: they were all part of our daily life.'

Daphne studied archaeology at the University of Malta, and was already working as a journalist as she studied. What made this particularly unusual, says her sister, was that she wrote under her own name. 'Newsrooms were very male-dominated and very staid; reporting was very literal; there were no bylines, no opinion columnists, no analysts . . . nothing.' Daphne's approach was different: she started up a column called 'The Good, The Bad, and The Ugly'. From the outset, there was an element of revealing wrongdoing in public office.

According to Mario Xuereb, Daphne could write just about anything. 'Straitjackets didn't suit her.' What she excelled in and received plaudits for were 'investigative and well-researched theses . . . She was even called a "One-woman Wikileaks". But she could also write what you could term as gossip, and with her style of writing she made some enemies, especially among the political and the big-business class.'

Her sister recounted how she often received threats for relatively minor things. Notes were pinned to her door. Her dog was killed. People would take offence at what she had written, and 'their only way of acting, or taking revenge, was to issue a threat'. Perhaps this inured her to the danger: 'When you receive a threat for writing something relatively benign, you know, it gets less scary to take on bigger people who can actually do things.' So she took those threats in her stride. These weren't one-offs; even the killing of her dog happened more than once.

But she was, as Mario Xuereb says, 'a very brave woman, and a very brave journalist. She was never afraid of mentioning people, mentioning names, of listing names and of publishing photos on her blog.' The fact that she published these on her own personal blog, of course, also meant that she had no protection.

Many people took her to court. According to her sister, when she died there were forty-two pending cases against her, 'most of them involving people in power, or people close to them. It seems like all of those cases are somehow designed, or coordinated, or intended to inconvenience her to the point where she might eventually give up.' But giving up doesn't seem to have been something she ever considered. As Mario Xuareb says, 'Her criticism of government made her very unpopular, especially among the grassroots of the

Labour Party.' She did not shy away from criticising the party and its leaders. 'People from the Labour Party will tell you: "Daphne doesn't like us, so we don't like her."'

The Panama Papers were an important source of information for Daphne's stories. Using them, she was able to make allegations about people at the highest levels of the Maltese government. Did she pause before doing so, or did she feel that it was her duty to publish them straight away? Her sister is clear that if she was sure of her information, she would publish; she reported without fear or favour.

So soon after her death, Mario Xuereb was understandably unwilling to speculate about the motive behind the particular car bomb that targeted Daphne. But, as he says, there was no shortage of stories on her online archive about people who might have wanted her dead. 'Daphne herself, in one of her blogs, this time last year, had written about what she considered to be a pattern that was emerging: she wrote that "Visa smugglers are blown up by bombs in their cars while drug traffickers are shot by hitmen."'

Her sister echoes the idea that the answer to her murder lies within her body of work. Her journalism was informed from top to bottom by a need to champion the vulnerable, not just the poor or destitute, but any ordinary person not in power. 'In a country which doesn't function as a normal democracy should ... People can do things with impunity. I mean her own death was designed to be a spectacular act of impunity. There was no attempt to make it look like an accident.'

The immediate public reaction to her murder was shock and disbelief. Thousands of people gathered to demand justice and an investigation into it. Mario Xuereb, in summing up, paints a picture of a society in shock: 'The nation went into mourning, civil society called for justice, journalists called for more safeguards ... the nation is still mourning Daphne, and still waiting for answers.'

Postscript:

Those answers have not yet fully emerged. In 2019 businessman Yorgen

Fenech was arrested as a person of interest in the case. He has denied the charges against him. In 2021 Vincent Muscat was jailed after pleading guilty to his part in the killing, and, separately, an independent judicial enquiry ruled that the government was responsible for allowing a 'climate of impunity' in the state that allowed her to be killed. The following year brothers George and Alfred DiGiorgio were each sentenced to forty years in prison after pleading guilty to the murder. Meanwhile, the Daphne Project, a worldwide consortium of journalists from eighteen different news organisations, was set up to investigate the stories she was working on when she was killed.

Asma Jahangir

Born 27 January 1952; died 11 February 2018, aged sixty-six

Asma Jahangir was a human rights lawyer from Pakistan who risked her life to stand up for women and minorities. She was the founding chairwoman of the Human Rights Commission of Pakistan and served as the first female president of the country's Supreme Court Bar Association. Asma Jahangir cut her legal teeth defending her father, a left-wing politician, who was often imprisoned for opposing Pakistan's military dictators.

This is how Asma summed up the challenges facing women in Pakistan: 'Mostly I have heard people say that there is a glass ceiling through which you have to go, but my experience was it wasn't a glass ceiling, it was an *iron* ceiling!'

For *Last Word*, Matthew Bannister spoke about Asma to the writer Mohammed Hanif, a former head of the BBC's Urdu service. He started by outlining the role that Asma Jahangir played: 'For the last forty years she was a one-woman political opposition party in Pakistan.' This was in response at first to the military dictatorship that the country lived under in the 1980s. Asma was a founder member of the Women's Action Forum. Asma herself described how this organisation had come about: 'We didn't see ourselves as gender-specific when we set out. To be very honest I didn't even see myself as taking any lead role.' However, the government was pushing through laws that Asma characterised as 'anti-women ... for example, a law of rape. I mean extramarital sex was made punishable, so the implication was that if you were raped, and you went to the police station, and they thought, "Well, you had consented to the act," you were arrested yourself.'

Her stance on such matters put her in direct danger and resulted in threats to her own life. In perhaps the most chilling episode, one of her clients was killed in her office. Asma's own description of this event is hair-raising, and illustrative of how important her work was: 'She [the woman] came into my office and said: "My parents are here, and they are here to murder me."' Reassurances came through that the parents only wanted a meeting, and that it was only the mother who would attend. 'The mother came with another person, went in the room and just shot her dead.' Asma described her own 'sense of failure and anger at myself' after this terrible crime.

The authorities, particularly the military authorities, didn't take kindly to what Asma doing: she was put under house arrest on a couple of occasions, and in 1983 was imprisoned. She believed that the security services had developed a plan to assassinate her. Mohammed Hanif says that all this opposition did nothing to stop her: 'During these forty years the authorities, especially the military authorities, had realised that it was very, very, difficult to scare her. She spoke quite candidly, she named names.'

This defiant spirit can be clearly seen in an incident that took place in 2005. In response to the fact that women runners were being beaten up by right-wing factions when they took part in the marathon, and the government's inaction, Asma decided to organise a women's marathon. 'This was a challenge to a government that was calling itself liberal. And that enraged them. And so to teach me a lesson, to humiliate me, they tore off my shirt.' The women around her covered her with her scarves to protect her. 'I sort of didn't realise ... I heard myself this policewoman saying: "I can't do it, I can't do it." And then I was told this man actually beat up the policewoman – there were a lot of intelligence people in plain clothes – and then put his hand himself at the back of my neck and tore the shirt.'

As to whether there has been progress in women's rights in Pakistan, Asma contrasted the atmosphere in the 1980s, when even to speak about women's rights was 'taboo' and anyone who did so was a 'promiscuous person who was defying all social and religious norms', with the newer outlook: 'Now, even the very right-wing religious parties address the question of women's rights, so we have come a long way there.'

Asma also campaigned on behalf of bonded workers, particularly brick-kiln workers. Mohammad Hanif explains why she took up their cause so energetically: 'There are some injustices in our society which happen out in the open. So these brick-kiln workers, everybody can see them, that these people live in utter poverty.' When Asma discovered that these workers were actually 'being treated like slaves, being bought and sold', she took them on as clients and fought their cases. 'And ... she made sure that she dragged those families into the courts, which made judges very uncomfortable, because they had never seen half-clothed people in the courts who could not read or write, who could not speak the language of the law. So, she literally got people out of slavery, thousands and thousands of people.'

His final analysis of Asma is simple: 'She showed us that these injustices happen in front of our eyes and we can't just look away and walk away.'

Or, in her own words: 'There have been times I have been scared, there have been times that I have cried, but does that mean that you give up in the face of brute force? No, never!'

Determined Women

Perhaps all of the women in this book could be described as determined. But there does seem to be a particular type of woman who gets things done through sheer force of character. In this section we meet those tenacious women who, by setting their minds to it, have raised ships or raised children, have spied for their country, broken records, undertaken adventures, and in one case even managed to move mountains.

They are irresistible, in more ways than one. But determination has a flip side. Among this spirited company, it comes as rather a shock to come face to face with the formidable and brutal Griselda Blanco, or even Lolita Lebrón – a heroine to some, a terrorist to others.

The tone of *Last Word* is more often celebratory than sad. But there are episodes where the loss of what might have been is the unavoidable top note. In this section we meet two determined women – Jo Cox and Dekha Ibrahim Abdi – whose lives were cut short before the full fruits of their work could be realised. It is hard not to wonder how much more these women might have achieved, given the chance. The dynamic image of Jo Cox that we are left with in the account conjured by her friend – leaning with enthusiasm into a conversation, scarf thrown over her shoulder, eager to change the world – reminds us that tenaciousness is a quality that should be harnessed, and celebrated.

Daphne Park,
Baroness Park of Monmouth

Born 1 September 1921; died 24 March 2010, aged eighty-eight

> *'In the Congo you could get hit on the head at any time, it was a matter of luck. There were times that were dicey, but I am an optimist. I always thought I would be there the next day.'*
>
> Baroness Daphne Park

Baroness Daphne Park was a female pioneer, one who rose through the ranks of the secret services and ended up in the House of Lords. She held diplomatic postings throughout the world, but the jobs were usually cover stories for her real career as an MI6 spy. She worked undercover in Moscow, Vietnam and the Belgian Congo. She survived many dangerous situations in the field and went on to become a MI6 controller, heading up covert operations in North and South America. Later she became a BBC governor and worked at Oxford University before joining the House of Lords as a life peer.

Daphne's own measured response when asked in an interview what makes a good spy was: 'You can't be a good one unless you trust, and you inspire trust. It is utterly wrong to think it is a world of betrayal. It is not, it is the exact opposite. And it is lively and fun, and you meet, of course, the most wonderful people.'

For *Last Word*, John Wilson spoke to another former secret agent turned baroness, Meta Ramsay, who met Daphne when the latter was quite senior and she herself was just joining the service. 'She had already been in the Congo, and in Zambia, both of which had been very exciting and very successful postings. She was just about to go to Hanoi and of course it was a time when North Vietnam was very much not a friendly place for us to be.'

Daphne herself described the rigours of life in Hanoi as an 'extremely uncomfortable existence', with, sometimes, 'very little food'. Part of her job was to talk to the Soviet ambassador, from whom she would get carefully imparted pieces of information 'that we didn't necessarily believe, but they were interesting to hear'.

Daphne didn't conform to the stereotypical image of the secret services. Though, as Meta Ramsay points out, 'if you do, you don't survive for very long. She was much more Miss Marple than James Bond.' She was famous in the Foreign Office for having described in a despatch a dinner she had given to the French ambassador 'while the rats played games round and round the pails that were laid out to catch the drips from the roof!'

Another tough posting was to the Belgian Congo, a highly volatile country at the time when she was there: 'Very dangerous,' says Meta Ramsay. 'It was a very, very bad time in the Congo.' This was a time of 'tremendous violence', there were roadblocks everywhere and 'an out-of-control army'. Daphne would drive her *deux chevaux* on her own, something that was 'not easy, but she got through by a great deal of wit, and in some cases charm, and in some cases just bravura performances'.

She used to talk about this herself with great insouciance, describing how she once smuggled someone out in the boot of her car. 'That was more risky for him than for me in a way. I must have been arrested and condemned to be shot several times, and it was a hazard that I got used to.'

Meta Ramsay describes how Daphne was once stopped at a roadblock. When asked to get out she refused, having taken the lie of the land. 'So they then decided that they would pull her physically out. Daphne was always quite well rounded, never very slim, so they tried to take her out through the sunshine roof and she stuck. And then she started to laugh, and then they all laughed, and so instead of killing her, or attacking her, or doing whatever they thought they were going to do her, they just laughed and laughed and eventually tried to sort things out and she went on her way.' Her warmth and sense of humour seem to have saved her.

After three decades in government service as a diplomat, an MI6 controller and secret agent, in 1980 Daphne Park took up a new role as principal of Somerville College, Oxford. At a social event she introduced herself to Mary Warnock, now Baroness Warnock: 'She didn't at first say that she had come to be principal of Somerville, and she certainly didn't look like my idea of the principal of Somerville, because her predecessor had been very tall and willowy, and Daphne was the opposite of that.' They spoke together about Moscow, 'so I assumed that she had been at the embassy and that she was a diplomat. She was very funny, and I really enjoyed it, but I had no idea that she wasn't a regular member of the Foreign Office. It wasn't for ages that I found out that she was a spy.'

In 1990 Daphne Park was made a life peer and became Baroness Park of Monmouth. Meta Ramsay, now Baroness Ramsay of Cartvale, remembers her time in the House of Lords, where they formed a bond, based perhaps on a shared experience of being in the field in the services. They found themselves often in coalition on the issues that mattered to them, although they were on different sides of the House.

Baroness Warnock recollects her as 'fearless really. I think she was essentially a brave person.' Towards the end of her life she lost mobility, but would whizz around the House of Lords in her motorised wheelchair. She was a popular figure, says Meta Ramsay, 'because most people knew her background and therefore admired her. And if you listened to her when she stood up and spoke, and you listened to the content of what she said, you realised that you were listening to a great deal of experience and wisdom.' She might have looked a bit like Miss Marple or a maiden aunt, 'but nobody could fail to take her seriously once they heard her speak'.

Lolita Lebrón

Born 19 November 1919; died 1 August 2010, aged ninety

Mass crowds turned out on the streets of San Juan in August 2010 to celebrate the life of the woman known simply to Puerto Ricans as 'Doña Lolita', or Lolita Lebrón. That she lived to ninety was a surprise, even to her. She didn't expect to live beyond 1 March 1954, the day that she led a gun attack on the US House of Representatives, which wounded several Congressmen and saw her jailed for the next twenty-five years. The former beauty queen from Puerto Rico soon became the poster-woman for the nationalist struggle to gain independence from the USA, and she is often now compared to revolutionaries such as Che Guevara and Pancho Villa.

For *Last Word*, Jane Little spoke to one of Lolita's co-conspirators, Rafael Miranda, who spent many years in solitary confinement on the island of Alcatraz. He began by describing her as someone who was 'very beautiful ... physically speaking, and a woman with beauty inside'. She was also defined by her love for her country, and by wanting to defend it against the humiliation and exploitation that she saw there. 'Lolita Lebrón was a woman with much love in her heart.' As for the events of March 1954? 'She went there really to die.'

Angelo Falcón, an analyst of the country, describes how in 1954 Puerto Rico was at a turning point in its history as it moved from being more or less a colony of the USA to being part of a commonwealth. To the nationalists, however, this was the same thing. Their aim in March was attention-grabbing. They weren't out to kill anyone; they wanted to make a statement. However, they did believe that they would not be coming home, 'that they were going to be killed in that action'. As one of the participants, Rafael Miranda backs this up: 'We all knew what to expect there in Washington, and we were ready for it.' He recalls Lolita entering the Capitol calmly, 'with dignity; she was in control of herself'.

The revolutionaries – Lolita leading three men – went into the visitors' gallery of the House of Representatives, sat down and opened fire from there, shouting 'Free Puerto Rico'. In the ensuing shooting, five Congressmen were hit. Rafael stresses that Lolita was firing at the ceiling rather than at the Congressmen: 'The bullet – her bullet – was still there.' There was an element of chaos to it all.

If they had set out to grab attention, they had succeeded. In 1954, before the women's liberation movement, the fact that a woman – let alone a 'very petite, very well-dressed woman' – had taken a leading role was unexpected. It was an image that captured the imagination of many, both at home and abroad.

The repercussions in Puerto Rico were immediate, says Angelo Falcón. The US government promptly stepped in and took repressive steps in Puerto Rico. 'The head of the Nationalist Party was arrested, as were sympathisers across the United States. It was a very, very dramatic day.'

After they were arrested there was a high-profile trial. Lolita emphasised throughout that she never intended to kill anyone. When asked in subsequent interviews whose plan this had been, Lolita was emphatic: 'It was my idea, and our idea, all of ours idea.' She was convicted and sentenced to between sixteen and fifty years, the longest term possible. She served this in a women's prison, spent time in solitary confinement and became very religious. She didn't regret her actions because, says Rafael Miranda, 'You don't really care when you do something for love.'

Twenty-five years later President Jimmy Carter granted her clemency. After that she returned to Puerto Rico, where, says Angelo Falcón, 'she became basically an advocate for peace', advocating non-violent protest.

As to whether she is seen as revolutionary hero or a terrorist, Angelo Falcón believes the answer is complex: 'She is seen as both ... Some people see her as a freedom fighter or hero, a symbol of Puerto Rican nationalism; others see her as a terrorist, as some-one who embarrassed the Puerto Rican people, who brought upon our community a wave of repression in the 1950s.'

Her death itself brought this history back into focus. Angelo Falcón considers that it gave the Puerto Rican people, and espe-cially the younger generations, 'kind of a teachable moment'. Her death prompted young people who didn't know much about her to understand a chapter of Puerto Rican history and revisit what happened in March 1954. Her legacy perhaps is to strengthen the Puerto Rican identity, imbuing it with a kind of 'gentle nationalism'. The recurring phrase was 'She is Puerto Rico.' 'To many people in Puerto Rico, she is the embodiment of what it means to be a Puerto Rican, of what it means to be a nation.'

Rafael Miranda is more emotional in his summing-up: 'To me she was not dead, people like that don't die. I don't feel sorry that she died, because I am glad that she lived!'

Christiane Desroches Noblecourt

Born 17 November 1913; died 23 June 2011, aged ninety-seven

Christiane Desroches Noblecourt was a French Egyptologist who played a leading role in saving the ancient temples of Nubia from the encroaching waters of the Aswan Dam. Her audacious plan involved dismantling these important historic monuments stone by stone and then moving them to higher ground, a feat which, as this episode of Last Word *makes clear, everybody else thought was almost inconceivable.*

Christiane was inspired to study Egyptology by magazine articles about the discovery of Tutankhamun's tomb in the 1920s. After taking a course at the Louvre Museum in Paris, she joined the French Institute of Oriental Archaeology in Cairo. For *Last Word*, Matthew Bannister spoke to Olga Prud'homme, a film-maker who made a documentary about Christiane's work. She points out that Christiane was pioneering as a woman working in the predominantly male sphere of archaeology, where men did not accept her easily. It was a tough situation. The sense of being a woman in a masculine world obviously went deep. Her former colleague in Cairo, Dr Faiza Heikal, remembers their first meeting: 'The first encounter we had was a bit funny because she said: "Oh you know I don't like to work with women," and I said: "Nor do I." And then, since I speak French, she decided that she liked me.' She was, Dr Heikal says, 'a very, very, strong person, very dynamic, motivated and motivating for the people who were working with her'.

Olga Prud'homme underlines Christiane's extraordinary force of will: 'When she decided something she would go for it, whatever happened around her.' It was this quality that allowed her to imagine the possibility of saving the temples of Nubia. One of the biggest challenges was to save the temple at Abu Simbel created by Rameses the Great in around 1250 BC in honour of his wife, Nefertari. Only Christiane believed that the 20-metre-high figures cut into solid rock could be moved. She approached the task with characteristic determination, as her own account shows: when everybody said, 'We can't save it! ... It is finished, we leave it', her response was the exact opposite: 'I say: "No, no, France will save it."' The problem was, of course, money.

The idea of moving the temples wholesale, from one place to another, must have struck many people as almost impossible: Olga Prud'homme describes it as 'crazy' to move the temples piece by piece. Very few people would have thought it possible or fought for it to happen.

Nevertheless, Christiane promised that the French government would help to fund the operation, overlooking the fact that she hadn't yet asked the president, Charles de Gaulle. When she did, he was outraged. She said to him: 'Générale, when you were in London, close to Churchill, when he gave you the BBC to speak, who asked you to do that? Nobody.' He laughed, and responded, 'You are right.' And then he gave her the money.

Of course, as Olga Prud'homme points out, 'Alone she could do nothing, so she knew that it had to go on an international level.' She approached UNESCO, and slowly, bit by bit, she managed to persuade people, and the shared conviction that the project was possible took hold.

Abu Simbel is a huge and awe-inspiring piece of work. The challenge involved in moving the giant figures was immense. It was a painstaking process. Dr Faiza Heikal describes Christiane as 'the dynamo of the whole event. She had a tremendous energy, she could work more than average people; so many hours running without getting fatigued ... she never missed anything.'

The operation was a success, though it took in total twenty years. When it was complete, Christiane's own words give a sense of the extraordinary conjuring trick that had been pulled off: 'I thought – Philae has not been moved, the monuments are so nicely rebuilt and so complete.'

It was thanks to Christiane's efforts that UNESCO established the idea of World Heritage Sites, an idea that has now spread around the world. Olga Prud'homme underlines the importance of this concept. It was, she says 'really the first act of consciousness that there is a history that we all share, all human beings'.

Christiane's successor as head of Egyptology at the Louvre Museum in Paris is Guillemette Andreu. For her, the feat that Christiane undertook was literally 'moving the mountains – in French we say: *remuer les montagnes*. It means that impossible is possible.'

A poignant detail from Olga Prud'homme captures the extent of Christiane's extraordinary achievement: the moment that Christiane felt she had succeeded in her mission was the day she saw that the birds which used to nest in the temple at Abu Simbel had come back. 'They came back,' she said, 'once the temple had been rebuilt.'

Dekha Ibrahim Abdi

Born 1964; died 14 July 2011, aged forty-six

Dekha Ibrahim Abdi, who died in a car crash aged forty-six, won international awards for her work as a peacemaker. The Kenyan-born Muslim was praised for her skill in bringing together warring factions from different tribes and different religions. She was much in demand in divided countries like Cambodia, Somalia, South Africa, Israel, Zimbabwe and Ethiopia.

But her skills were tested to the limit after the presidential elections in her native Kenya in 2007. Following the accession of President Mwai Kibaki in December of that year, more than 120 people were killed in an outbreak of violence prompted by dissatisfaction with the result and with Kibaki's precipitate swearing-in ceremony.

As soon as the election results came out, Dekha brought together a group, Concerned Citizens for Peace. Carolyn Hayman, of the charity Peace Direct, describes their modus operandi as reaching out as broadly as possible – they would invite anyone who had any information about where violence was breaking out to come to the room they had hired in a Nairobi hotel. From there, they were inventive, taking as many approaches as they could. For instance, they came to an arrangement with mobile phone companies so that anybody calling the company would get a recorded message saying 'Violence is not the answer.' They encouraged vice-chancellors at the universities to speak to their students and persuade them to go back to university. 'For the first three weeks of the uprising . . . Concerned Citizens for Peace were at the centre of attempts to calm down the violence.'

Dekha Ibrahim Abdi was born in the Wajir region of Kenya, at a time when the area was under emergency law as the government tried to crush a pro-Somali rebellion. She recalled living with dawn-to-dusk curfews and failing to sit an important exam because her family had to flee from fighting. In her adult life, Dekha worked with others to bring together the many different warring factions in Wajir, becoming the secretary of the Regional Peace Committee; but Carolyn Hayman says it wasn't just her own experience that led Dekha into conflict resolution. Surprisingly, Dekha told her that her first inspiration came from reading about the Dutch family who had sheltered Anne Frank. Dekha's own achievements took a different form, but there was the sense that she was inspired by the way that 'people can be incredibly brave when the situation requires'. Her drive to stand up and do what was necessary went right back to when she got involved in the conflict in Wajir, very early on in her life. This attitude certainly wasn't expected of a woman, and probably came with a level of personal danger, 'because women weren't expected to galvanise the tribal elders into acting and that was quite a controversial move: they were told, you know: "You are women, what do you know about this?"'

Dekha's own view of what she was trying to achieve by bringing as many different groups together was to try to find ways in which 'people from differences – either clan differences, political differences, religious differences' could find common ground and mutual ways of working. Her aim was to get people to understand diversity – 'not as a problem, but as a strength'.

Dekha's younger brother, Mohamed Abdi, spoke to Matthew Bannister for *Last Word*, describing what Dekha was like as a person and what it was that drove her. He spoke of her as a 'natural leader', an attribute that she had had since she was a child. It was an integral and spontaneous part of her character. But she was also a woman with humility, a quality that allowed her to connect with all the people she came in contact with. For Mohamed, the value of her work cannot be overstated: 'In the Islamic religion it is believed that if you save a soul you have saved the whole world. So that is the kind of perspective she has been working on, saving lives, bringing peace, bringing harmony within the community.'

In 2005, Carolyn Hayman invited Dekha to come to London to talk to young Muslims in the wake of the 7/7 suicide bombings. This was a tense time for Muslim people, and Dekha's approach was to challenge them, saying: 'Don't be sorry for yourself because you feel people are against you. You have to take the initiative to go out, and mix with broader British society.' She was clear in setting out where she felt their responsibilities lay. Her charisma and personality were qualities that allowed her to 'challenge people to do more than they perhaps felt able to do'.

Dekha herself stressed the importance of engagement with '*all* groups around the world, especially with Muslim groups, who are now seen as the bad in the world'. Having been brought up with the notion that people should stick to their own, her strong belief came by understanding that 'the learning comes by engaging with the other'.

Carolyn Hayman highlights that this was never going to be an easy task: 'Making peace is not ... a peace and love and doves kind of thing at all. It is a very strenuous, very hard work, a blood, sweat and tears kind of activity.' Dekha threw herself into this work with great force. But she never lost sight of where she came from. As Carolyn says, it is only too easy 'for people who get on the international circuit to lose contact with their roots, and sometimes to become self-important, and Dekha never did that. Her whole life was about service.'

But in the aftermath of her death, it is perhaps the family's voice, that of her brother Mohamed, which should have the last word, describing how his sister was more than a sister to him. She was his confidante, his support: 'I have lost a very big help on my side. I find my side very empty, now.'

Nusrat Bhutto

Born 23 March 1929; died 23 October 2011, aged eighty-two

Begum Nusrat Bhutto was the matriarch of Pakistan's most prominent political dynasty. Her husband, Zulfikar Ali Bhutto, was the country's first democratically elected leader. When he was ousted in a military coup by General Zia in 1977, she became co-chairman of the Pakistani People's Party, or PPP, which he had founded. She led the party until her daughter Benazir took over in the mid-1980s. Her life was mired by tragedy, with her husband hanged in 1979 and the loss of three of her children.

Matthew Bannister spoke to Pakistan's commissioner in London, Wajid Shamsul Hasan, a long-standing friend of Mrs Bhutto, who explained that Nusrat was originally from a prominent and prosperous family from Iran. She herself was brought up firstly in India, and then moved to Karachi when she was a teenager. It was in Karachi that she met the man who was to be her husband, Zulfikar Ali Bhutto: 'It was love at first sight.'

The Pakistani novelist Kamila Shamsie spoke to *Last Word*, describing Nusrat as 'an extremely glamorous woman. In every picture you see of her she is looking very beautiful and svelte in a sari, with her hair impeccably done.' The perception of her was that she was 'a very good First Lady ... the gracious hostess'. Which meant that when General Zia took over in the coup of 1977, 'I think a lot of people were probably quite surprised to see her taking up the role of chairperson of the Pakistan People's Party and doing it with such fierceness.'

After the coup, 400 PPP officials were arrested, and Nusrat had to wait for the Supreme Court of Pakistan to decide whether or not her husband should be executed. It must have been a horrific time for her, but she was of course steadfast in her support, describing him at the time as a 'great man' who would 'go down in history' if he were to be hanged. He was indeed executed on 4 April 1979.

This event of course marked a huge change in her life as she took up his political mantle. As Kamila Shamsie points out, she went from being a kind of Jackie Kennedy figure to an activist, being seen 'at some political rally, police with batons coming after her; it was a completely different kind of woman that actually emerged at that point'. Wajid Shamsul Hasan describes her political philosophy as 'secular, liberal, progressive'. She was concerned with 'empowerment of the people, empowerment of women, empowerment of minorities'.

The political life in Pakistan was not for the faint-hearted. Wajid Shamsul Hasan describes an episode at a rally when Nusrat was baton-charged by police. She lost a great deal of blood as the injury was not seen to quickly, and it 'had a lasting effect on her life'. To take up the role she did meant that she had to be a hugely courageous woman, he says, 'because that was the time when everybody would surrender at the first sound of the whip'. PPP supporters were 'being prosecuted, hanged, publicly whipped' and going to jail. In this fractious political atmosphere, she was spied on by the government. When asked in an interview about this, she said wryly: 'I have been followed here today by two motorcyclists, one jeep, and one Fiat car, full of their own hounds. Bloodhounds, I call them.'

The Bhutto family, prominent as they were in Pakistani politics, also attracted tragedy, says Kamila Shamsie: 'So in '79 her husband was executed. A few years later her son Shahnawaz died under mysterious circumstances. Then you have her eldest son Murtaza being killed.' Lastly, her daughter Benazir was assassinated in 2007. 'Very quickly what started to happen was you started to associate her with these terrible deaths and losses. By the end of her life, in some very sad way people had started to forget that she had been a significant political figure.' Instead, she was seen as a woman who had lost her children and her husband in 'all sorts of horrible ways'.

The concept of a political dynasty is a strong one in Pakistani politics, as outlined by Nusrat Bhutto herself: 'Military coups d'état never last long. We are a family of politicians: he goes, his son will come, his daughter will come, his grandson, his granddaughter, they will take over.' This dynastic element is not uncontroversial. It could be viewed as anti-democratic for one family to so dominate the leadership of a political party. Wajid Shamsul Hasan himself acknowledges this, but also points to other countries and dynasties – the Kennedys, the Bushes, the Gandhis.

Asked to sum up Nusrat Bhutto's contribution, Kamila Shamsie also points to the familial nature of the PPP: 'The important legacy was right when her husband died ... to take on that role of chairperson of the PPP.' There was a perception that she was holding on to this role 'until Benazir was old enough to do it, but I think that's unfair to her'.

At the time of her death, not only was her son-in-law president of Pakistan, but her grandson was the co-chair of the party with his father, as Kamila Shamsie points out: 'The Pakistan People's Party is very much seen as the Bhutto party. It is not something I am uncritical of, but that is the way it is, and we have yet to see about his sisters. The Bhutto women, as we know, are no shrinking violets, they have taken part in the political system and they may choose to take up a role. And I don't think anyone thinks that the Bhuttos are about to exit stage-left any time soon.'

Griselda Blanco

Born 15 February 1943; died 3 September 2012, aged sixty-nine

The Colombian gangster Griselda Blanco was known as the 'cocaine godmother'. She built a multi-million-dollar business out of smuggling drugs into the USA, using extreme violence to protect her empire. She even continued to control it when she was serving a prison sentence. Eventually she was deported back to Colombia, where she was shot dead.

The film-maker Alfred Spellman made a documentary about Blanco, and told Matthew Bannister for *Last Word* that her story was like an episode of the TV series *Miami Vice*. He described a Colombian childhood characterised by poverty and overshadowed by the civil war that was known as '*La Violencia*', a conflict that claimed the lives of tens of thousands of people. Griselda got into the drug-trafficking trade early in her career, and in fact in 1974 was one of the first people to be indicted for cocaine trafficking in the USA.

Bob Palombo was the agent who made it his life's work to try to track Griselda down. She had been identified as one of the three main Colombian drug smugglers who were bringing cocaine and marijuana into New York. He was assigned as the principal agent on the case, 'and we began a lengthy wire-tap and surveillance'. As Alfred Spellman describes it, 'The police in Miami in the 1980s knew who she was, knew she was operating in South Florida. She had various homes, was a master of disguise, and she would be out in public, but she was hiding in plain sight.'

The first time Bob Palombo saw her for himself was at the Marriott Hotel in Newport Beach, California: 'She was dressed very smartly, in a dress, with a very fashionable light-brown frosty wig.' Her disguise as a generic, wealthy, upper-middle-class woman was so effective that when she first walked by the watching police didn't spot her. 'But she had this very distinctive cleft in her chin, and dimples on her cheek. When she walked by again, my partner and I both noticed the cleft, and the dimples, and we looked at each other and basically nodded.'

By this time, says Alfred Spellman, 'she had become known as one of the most violent operators in the cocaine business'. Part of that could be attributed to the fact that as a woman in 'what is traditionally a very macho business – she had to prove her mettle, so to speak'. And prove her mettle she did. Bob Palombo describes her effect on the homicide rate – with some estimates going as high as 250 victims. (Bob himself is more comfortable putting the figure at 'in excess of fifty to seventy-five homicides she was involved with'.) He wryly notes that 'After her arrest the homicide rate dropped dramatically.'

Griselda had initially set up in business with her husband, but, it is rumoured, went on to kill him. 'Three of her husbands have been murdered,' says Alfred Spellman 'and most people speculate that she was directly responsible, which got her the nickname "the Black Widow".'

She had pioneered the use of various smuggling techniques, including sending hundreds of kilos of drugs on the tall ship *Gloria* that sailed into New York from Colombia as part of the 1976 US Bicentennial celebrations. Bob Palombo describes her innovation of specially adapted underwear, using a factory she had an interest in to produce 'girdles and bras with concealed pockets'. 'Depending on the size of the individual smuggling, you could get as much as two to three kilos on a person.' Other innovations included murder techniques such as the idea of shooting the target from a motorcycle so that the killing could take place at close range and the murderer could quickly disappear into the traffic.

Griselda's reputation and financial success came at the price of being constantly on the move. According to Alfred Spellman, she moved from New York to Colombia, then to Miami and California.

It was there, after being a fugitive for about eleven years, that she was finally arrested.

By the time of her arrest, according to Bob Palombo, she had made so many enemies in South Florida that multiple people were on her tail, one of whom was a man called Jaime Bravo, the nephew of an ex-lover of hers. 'And Jaime Bravo became aware of the fact that she was allegedly responsible for the demise of his uncle Alberto Bravo, and he decided to gun for her.'

But it was Palombo who tracked her down first and arrested her. And when he did, he kissed her. The police had found out where she was and burst into the house. Alfred Spellman described the scene: 'She was lying in bed reading a Bible, and Special Agent Palombo went over to her and kissed her on the cheek.'

There was a neat symbolism to this action: he had made a promise over the long years of hunting for her that 'if I ever chase her down, I am going to plant a kiss on her cheek – like the kiss of death that the Italians did back in the organised crime days'. He was drawing on his own Italian heritage, though, as he admits, she was probably happier to see the police arrive than she would have been to see Jaime Bravo.

She spent nineteen years in prison, and on her release in 2004 was immediately deported back to Colombia, where, unsurprisingly, she had legions of enemies. She was under threat right from the moment she landed. 'Most people speculated that she wouldn't make it out of the airport,' says Albert Spellman. In the end it took a while, but 'Griselda Blanco ended up getting murdered in broad daylight, as she was leaving a butcher's shop.'

As Bob Palombo puts it: 'She died, like she lived, a violent death – kind of poetic justice, if you will – a butcher, killed in a butcher's shop by a shooter using a technique that she developed. I don't honestly wish death on anybody, to include her. But if anybody deserved the ultimate punishment, it was Griselda Blanco.'

Fiona Gore, Countess of Arran

Born 20 July 1918; died 16 May 2013, aged ninety-four

The Countess of Arran was a champion powerboat racer who repeatedly broke records. She was born Fiona Colquhoun, the daughter of a baronet. In 1937 she married Sir Arthur Gore, known as 'Boofy'. He wrote a column in the London Evening News *while his wife pursued her love of speed. In 1958 he succeeded his brother to become the 8th Earl of Arran.*

Matthew Bannister spoke to their son, the current earl, for Last Word. *He described first of all her love of animals – her pets included the standard dogs, but also wallabies, llamas, pot-bellied pigs and Falabella horses. 'And I remember well the badgers . . . I had to go around in gumboots as a young boy, because the badgers always nipped one's heels the whole time and one got rather frightened of them.' On his parents' bed there would be a menagerie including a badger, a fox, a Jack Russell, an Alsatian and a Macaw parrot. 'The smell in there in the morning was just like a farmyard.'*

The countess was chiefly famous for her speed. Known as the 'World's Fastest Grandmother', or the 'Racing Countess', she reached speeds of more than 80 miles per hour in her boat the *Skean Dhu*. John Puddifoot, the manager of the powerboat division of the Royal Yachting Association, explains her records: 'She set a record in Class 1, at 82 miles an hour, and then another one the following year, in 1972, at 92 miles an hour.' Finally, she became the first woman to break the 100-mile-an-hour barrier when she set a record of 102 miles an hour. She was sixty-two at the time.

It's stuff that requires nerves of steel, a resource she was never short of – she described herself as a sixteen-year-old racing her car up and down the twisting roads on the side of Loch Lomond 'when the village policeman wasn't looking'. She said that the love of speed was just innate in her: 'Where it came from, God only knows.'

Her family got used to taking it for granted, says her son – their attitude was: 'Oh, Mummy's going racing again tomorrow. Good luck, Mummy.' His father was a very proud husband, sometimes using a helicopter to hover above her boat, much to her irritation. The current earl believes that she herself was probably most proud of her world record, set on Lake Winderere: 'She said, "I have done it for Scotland!"' Though according to an interview at the time of one of her record challenges, her main motivation was the avoidance of 'the sheer boredom of sitting at home and doing nothing'.

She was tremendously glamorous; John Puddifoot described her going racing 'in silver-lamé race suit, goggles, and it was like something out of the Hollywood films'. When the Yachting Association bought her boat from her, they discovered that there were three straws sticking up from the dash panel in front of the driver. 'We looked around the back and they were labelled suitable beverages that undoubtedly would have assisted her in her racing at the time!' He was laughingly reluctant to name the beverages, but it clearly brought a smile to his face just to think about her.

But it is the Earl of Arran's last words on his mother that really sum up her character: 'You know, she had everything, my mother, there was no weakness in her. And, whatever she did, she just got it *right*.'

Beryl Platt,
Baroness Platt of Writtle

Born 18 April 1923; died 1 February 2015, aged ninety-one

Beryl Platt was a wartime aeronautical engineer who, in her words, 'staggered' her colleagues on her first day at work simply because she was a woman. She went on to pursue a career in local government, served for twenty years on Essex County Council, and was made a life peer in 1981, becoming Lady Platt of Writtle. Two years later she was appointed chair of the Equal Opportunities Commission. She also campaigned to promote women in science and engineering. Throughout her life she had a reputation for boundless energy and getting things done.

Her daughter Vicky told Julian Worricker for Last Word *that their childhood nickname for her was 'the Battleship of the Republic' because 'she used to go forward all guns blazing! And we children would be rocking around in her wake.' She characterises her mother as someone with a lot of vigour, energy and determination.*

Beryl Platt studied aeronautical engineering at Girton College, Cambridge, and then joined the Hawker Aircraft Company in its experimental flight test department. That meant secret work on fighters such as the Tempest, the Typhoon and the Hurricane. Her own words describing this time give a sense of the level of expertise involved: 'I was writing flight reports for their flight test department, starting with first flights and really very secret aircraft.' The test pilot would fly the single-seater fighters with a roller pad on his knee, and when he came down 'I had to write the flight report and then correct the test figures to standard temperature and pressure, so we knew the rate of climb, high speed and length of take-off of the aircraft.' Vicky Platt explains the pride her mother took in this work: with regard to the Hurricanes, she really felt a part of their success (it was said that 60 per cent of air battles were won by these planes). Or as Beryl herself put it, 'We really thought that we were helping to win the war,' a sentiment that was reinforced when a telegram arrived at the department from Sir Stafford Cripps, Minister of Aircraft Production, crediting their efforts.

After the war she worked on air safety for British European Airways, giving up her job when she married in 1949. Then, having moved to Writtle in her native Essex, she became active in local government. Vicky describes her fearless nature and how she deployed it, for example in fighting off an attempt by a property developer to build on the Writtle Recreation Grounds. In the end, confronted by Beryl's opposition, 'he sold the playing fields to the parish council for a pound'.

Her next move was on to the Equal Opportunities Commission. Margaret Thatcher offered her the job, which she was initially hesitant about because it had been so long – thirty years – since she had had a role of that sort. But equal opportunities was a cause close to her heart, 'something she believed in deeply'. There was also a feeling that her own career in engineering had been affected by the difficulties at the time of working after having children. This was a chance for her to make a difference, and 'push forward opportunities for women in science and engineering'.

Marie-Noelle Barton is a former director of WISE – Women in Science and Engineering – an organisation that Beryl co-founded in the 1980s, and she explains the importance of what Beryl was trying to achieve. There was a sense that some women were more likely to pull up the drawbridge after themselves, reasoning that because they hadn't had to rely on outside help, there was no need to help anyone else. 'But Beryl would take them through it in this analytical way, explaining that it wasn't just for the good of women – obviously it *was* for the good of women, because we didn't want women to miss out on such an exciting profession – but also explaining that it was for the good of industry.' Her point was that by only recruiting men, industry was restricting itself to less than half of the population. To get the best, she argued, 'you needed to recruit from 100 per cent of the population'.

Beryl was adamant about the need to make sure that girls remain engaged with mathematics and science. 'I think mothers have a good deal to do in this, that they must say to their daughters, just as much as they say to their sons: "No, I am sorry, you have *got* to understand it, you can't say that girls can't read a plan, or do a percentage, or whatever it is: they have got to do it too."'

A couple of vignettes give a wonderful sense of Beryl's practical and can-do character. The first comes from Vicky, who describe how her mother would steam into Hamley's toy shop, 'which had divided toys into sections: one for girls and one for boys'. Chemistry sets and science toys would be in the boys' department, while the girls' department would be filled with 'pink fluffy stuff'. Beryl would point out that they were losing sales, encouraging them to think about the possibilities, about how they could reorganise things. She would point out to employers that they were losing trained employees once they had had children. Her aim was always to encourage people and businesses to look at things differently.

Just as evocative of her commitment to science and engineering is the description from Marie-Noelle Barton of the contents of Beryl's handbag: 'She always had a screwdriver in her handbag. I was at a school with her once, and we were having a meeting and we were sitting next to a window and the window was draughty; and when they were serving coffee, and there was a bit of break, she got up and she said to me: "I am going to fix that window!" And she got her screwdriver out and fixed the window! She was very down to earth, was Beryl.'

Frances Kelsey

Born 24 July 1914; died 7 August 2015, aged 101

Frances Kelsey was a Canadian scientist and doctor who became a national heroine in America. She worked as a pharmacologist at the University of Chicago, where in the 1930s she first witnessed the effects of the lax regulation of new drugs. She and her colleagues identified a fatal ingredient that was being routinely added to an antibiotic to make it more palatable; their findings led to tighter legislation. But it was when she joined the Food and Drug Administration, or FDA, in Washington that she made her real impact, resisting pressure to pass the drug thalidomide.

The journalist Adam Bernstein from the **Washington Post** *spoke to Reeta Chakrabarti for* **Last Word** *and explained how thalidomide was being called a miracle drug, one that could cure morning sickness and insomnia. 'Women all over the world began taking it, except in the USA. It took a couple of years before scientists were able to realise that a great number of babies were being born with severe, severe, deformities; we are talking about missing limbs, ears, eyes, other internal organs. Tissues really failed to develop properly. So it was a horrific, horrific, story.' But this tragedy was on the whole averted in the USA.*

That was down, in large part, to Frances Kelsey. Her background was as a pharmacologist and also a medical doctor, at a time when science was still an unusual career for a woman. In around 1960 she joined the FDA, becoming one of seven medical officers who had to investigate around 300 cases every year.

Her involvement with thalidomide came very early on. In fact it was her first case, and they gave it to her, she said, because she was so inexperienced: they thought it was going to be an 'easy one' to start her off on. Three officials – herself, a pharmacologist and a chemist – were asked to review the initial submission, and came to the conclusion that it was inadequate. Adam Bernstein explains that 'she got very uncomfortable with the kinds of studies that had been performed. She thought they were incomplete, that important questions were not answered, and she immediately signalled to the drug company that there were big problems here.' And the drug company applied a lot of pressure on her to approve it. This pressure and her resistance went on for a long period – nineteen months; 'and those nineteen months are critical, because it was during that period that clinical investigators and scientists in other countries finally made the connection to the public health calamity of thalidomide'.

Eventually, President Kennedy himself would call for better-administered drug laws, and spoke out against the use of thalidomide. He rushed Frances into a ceremony honouring the heroes of the age.

She was perhaps an unexpected presence among the astronauts and other heroes, but as Adam Bernstein says, 'for that moment in time, she really was held up as the ideal bureaucrat'. It is rare that an official gets this kind of appreciation. But Adam Bernstein points out that even though she got a lot of attention for thalidomide, 'she actually had perhaps . . . a greater role *after* the thalidomide tragedy', because it was in the wake of this scandal and of her actions that the regulations that are still in force were properly hammered out: 'phased clinical trials, informed consent, drug companies *have* to warn the Food and Drug Administration about any adverse effects. It gave the FDA very important new controls over prescription drug advertising.' It is a legacy that continues to save lives.

Mary Ellis

Born 2 February 1917; died 24 July 2018, aged 101

Mary Ellis was one of the last surviving members of the wartime Air Transport Auxiliary. Mary and her colleagues delivered aeroplanes from factories to air bases all over the UK, often risking their lives: more than 160 women worked for the ATA and fifteen of them were killed on duty.

Mary's friend, the aviation historian Paul Beaver, spoke to Matthew Bannister for *Last Word*, and described how she got the 'flying bug' very early in her life, ever since she went on her first flight when she was only eight years old with a man called Sir Alan Cobham. Sir Alan would go round the country, land his plane on people's fields, and offer to take them up for a small amount of money to promote flying. When he landed on Mary's father's field near Brize Norton, he took her up and her obsession started from there. By 1937, at the age of around twenty, she was learning to fly in a light aircraft called a BA Swallow, and by the time the war started she was fully qualified and had her pilot's certificate.

The ATA, which comprised both men and women, existed to take the planes from the factories where they were made and ferry them to the operational stations. The excitement – and the fear – lay in the variety of aircraft that they had to fly. It called for a high level of proficiency, since the pilots would move straight from a Tiger Moth to a Wellington bomber or a Spitfire.

Paul Beaver explains how tricky this was: 'I can't believe, now, that we would allow such things. There was a lovely little handbook that ATA pilots had, which gave all the basic data. You really need what is called "the numbers"; to know the take-off speed, the stalling speed, you need to know the landing speed.' According to Paul Beaver, she was absolutely up to the challenge: she flew more than seventy-six types of aircraft, and made about 1,000 deliveries over the period of the war

There were, unsurprisingly, many male pilots who were shocked that the pilot delivering their aircraft was a woman, says Paul Beaver. There was one incident when Mary delivered a twin-engine bomber to an airfield. When she got out of it, 'somebody said: "Well, where's the pilot?"' They were so incredulous that a woman was claiming to have flown the plane that they actually got inside it to discover the pilot for themselves, and as she put it with typical humour: 'Everybody was flabbergasted that a little girl like me could fly these big aeroplanes, all by oneself.'

After the war ended, Paul says, 'she was one of the first women in the world to fly a jet'. There was a period when the RAF were considering recruiting women from the ATA to be fighter pilots, and she flew a Meteor jet fighter. When they decided not to pursue this policy, she turned her hand to becoming a private taxi pilot. The landowner she worked for eventually bought an airfield, Sandown in the Isle of Wight, where she became the managing director. She married one of her colleagues there, Don Ellis, and they lived next to the airfield.

Paul recalls an episode three years before she died, when 'one of the Spitfires that she had delivered came back to visit her'. They knew it was one of 'her' aircraft because she had signed the door. That signature – which in those days was Mary Wilkins – had remained for all those years, even through the restoration process. She signed the door again. When they asked her 'Why did you sign the aircraft?', she said: 'Well, I rather thought some lovely pilot would see it and go: I wonder who that girl is, I better give her a call.'

We can give the last word to Mary herself, describing with glee what it was like to fly with the ATA : 'You could go up and play with the clouds, you know, and have great fun!'

Margaret Rule

Born 27 September 1928; died 9 April 2015, aged eighty-six

Margaret Rule was the archaeologist who supervised the raising of Henry VIII's flagship, the **Mary Rose,** *from the seabed under the waters of the Solent. The project began in the mid-1960s with virtually no money and became an ambitious and pioneering operation, culminating in the emergence of the warship from the sea, an event watched by millions on television. The* **Mary Rose,** *and the thousands of artefacts recovered from the wreck, are now housed in a purpose-built museum in Portsmouth.*

Rear-Admiral John Lippiett is chairman of the Mary Rose Trust. He spoke to Matthew Bannister for *Last Word*, explaining the significance of the vessel: it was 'probably the first warship of our standing navy, built over 500 years ago'. It sank off Portsmouth in 1545 and became covered by mud, which preserved it.

Dr Alex Hildred worked alongside Margaret Rule on the *Mary Rose* dive team, and she describes 'passion and determination' as the overriding characteristics of Margaret's personality. The passion was infectious, and 'the determination meant that she was visionary in everything she did – and that's what made the project successful'.

In the early days of the excavation there was uncertainty about everything: where the wreck was, even how much of it had survived. Alex Hildred describes a lot of it as 'just seabed-searching: the first application in England, certainly, of remote sensing technology, sub-bottom profiling and side-scan sonar'. At the time, Margaret herself was not experienced in working underwater: she didn't even dive, but stayed in the boat receiving information from the divers. This was frustrating enough for her to learn how to do so, Dr

Hildred says: 'Pretty soon, she realised that the only way she could do it was to learn to dive.'

As for the thrilling moment of discovery, there was an element of luck, as Margaret herself explained: they had in fact missed the intended search area, and were about 150 metres to its south; 'and Percy Ackland, who I always called our underwater gun dog, he came up, and whispered to me: "The timbers are down there, Margaret!"'

After the discovery of the site, the technical challenges of the excavation only multiplied. An interview at the time captured the difficulties: 'We are working eleven feet beneath the seabed, that's pretty deep, in a huge hole with a ship above you.' Alex Hildred describes Margaret, having now learned to dive, diving 'in the trickiest areas. If we were having a problem deciding something, she would come and do it.' She also spent her time reviewing the video runs that were made of the site. It is one of the challenges of underwater archaeology: 'The director can't look over your shoulder in a trench and see what's happening everywhere. You have to rely on feedback from individuals.'

But the finds they were making were more than worth the technical effort. A description she gave at the time vividly conjures the types of artefacts they were discovering: 'Leather shoes, seaman's combs, arrows, and fragments of a quiver which can be reconstructed.' These objects were of particular value because on land they would probably not have been preserved. Here the conditions had allowed their survival, and they were of course dated, because 'we know [they] got into the silt on 19 July 1545'.

Not only was this a logistically difficult and challenging operation, but there were huge legal and bureaucratic constraints to overcome. She fought these 'tenaciously', according to Rear-Admiral Lippiett, 'which was very much in her character'. The question arose as to who should take ownership of the find, and 'she persuaded the government and the Receiver of Wrecks to entrust this extraordinary collection into the hands of the Mary Rose Trust'.

The other battle she had to fight was over the physical protection of the site itself. Margaret outlined the difficulties involved in this in an interview in 2004: 'Initially there was no way, legally, of protecting the *Mary Rose* ... And so we never left marker buoys on site, we alerted all our fishermen friends to keep a watching eye on it.' Eventually, they applied for a lease from the Crown Estate commissioners which allowed them to 'defend our patch of mud'. According to Rear-Admiral Lippiett, the Protection of Wrecks Act came about because of the *Mary Rose* and Margaret's efforts to protect it and retain the rights to it.

As well as tackling government officials, Margaret also had to deal with unfounded stories appearing in the press, such as the rumour that a chest of coins had been stolen from the site. 'That is absolutely ludicrous!' said Margaret; 'I mean for people diving there every single day, for nine months of the year, not to notice that a chest has gone is just unbelievable.'

The moment when the *Mary Rose* was raised, in October 1982, was a heart-stopping one for Margaret and for the whole team. Her words to journalists at the time conjure up not only the enormity of the occasion but the spirit with which she undertook the massive project: 'We have worked night and day, and if the things all come true in the night, I am afraid, gentlemen, she will be recovered during the night,' she said, laughing with the gathered journalists about whether they should stay up or not: 'If I do, I don't see why you shouldn't too.'

When the ship was finally raised, as the press excitedly announced, it was the first time it had been seen in 437 years. Alex Hildred describes the atmosphere: 'Margaret was crying and everyone else was cheering ... It had been such a strain, and finally it was there ... And she was also very sad, so there was a sadness, there was a happiness, there was a relief.'

It was the culmination of what she had given her life to: as she herself said, 'If I had left her there ... I would have had a much less worried twenty years, but, secondly, I wouldn't have had the exciting life I have had meeting such tremendous people as a result of the *Mary Rose*.'

The last word on Margaret Rule goes to Rear-Admiral John Lippiett, summing up her legacy. 'She was an extraordinary woman, full of resolve, tenacity. Her determination was to achieve against the odds when so many people would have said "This is not possible." She would never take no as the answer.'

Jo Cox

Born 22 June 1974; died 16 June 2016, aged forty-one

The brutal death of MP Jo Cox left the country in shock. She was shot and stabbed in the street after going about her constituency business in the West Yorkshire town of Birstall, where she had been MP for only a year.

Jo Cox described herself as 'a proud Yorkshire lass' who returned to her roots to represent Batley and Spen after university at Cambridge and a career built on working for charities. She left behind a husband, two small children and a political future full of promise. In a week where tributes to her poured in, this episode of *Last Word* gave a flavour of some of them, including that of her friend, the Labour MP Rachel Reeves, who emphasised her passion, energy and commitment: 'She always put you at ease, she always made you feel special.' She emphasised too the areas that Jo prioritised – issues local to Batley and Spen, but also international development, for which she drew on her time with Oxfam.

The voices of some of her constituents echo similar sentiments: 'She was someone who had a heart of gold, she really went beyond and going the extra mile to support local businesses and the community around here.'

'Nobody was singled out for her, she represented everybody. If you were Asian, like myself, white, black, she was there for you.'

Her maiden speech in the House of Commons – direct, humane, proud and compassionate – gives a sense of why she was so valued: 'Batley and Spen is a gathering of typically independent, no-nonsense, proud Yorkshire towns and villages. And while we celebrate our diversity, the thing that surprises me time and time again, as I travel around the constituency, is that we are far more united and have far more in common than that which divides us.' It also demonstrated that she wasn't afraid to be a little bit irreverent: 'Of course, Batley is a town that has sent Labour MPs to this place for the best part of 100 years. One of those, Dr Broughton, is of course famously credited with bringing down a government, so I respectfully put the right honourable members on the front bench opposite on notice.'

For *Last Word*, Reeta Chakrabarti spoke to Kate Proctor, the Westminster correspondent for the *Yorkshire Post*, who immediately pointed to Jo's sense of pride in Yorkshire and in her background. 'She was from a working-class family, she was the first in her family to go to university . . . she was very, very, proud to represent the area where she grew up.' Or as Jo herself put it in her maiden speech: 'I'm proud that I was made in Yorkshire; and I'm proud of the things we make in Yorkshire, and Britain should be proud of that too.'

Cambridge University was a great contrast to her Yorkshire upbringing, according to Kate Proctor: 'I don't think she felt she'd fitted in entirely at the beginning. She said she made great friends there, loved her course, but it was a massive shock to her and she said to me it shook her foundations . . . she realised that it was a very different world from having grown up in Batley and Spen.' She was upfront about the class differences she came up against at university, cleaving mostly to friends who were also from the north, and it was there that her political opinions started to form.

In all the many tributes that were paid to her in the aftermath of her death, there is a lot of talk about her principles. She was somebody who had a vision and wanted to change things, says Kate Proctor: 'She was a really interesting MP in that she always switched between constituency issues and national issues, but what united both of those things was the fact that she wanted to give people a voice – people who she felt weren't being heard, or people that were powerless to give across their views or to explain their plight.' The Syrian refugee crisis was one cause she became heavily involved in, speaking up on the need to bring refugees to Britain. She was also involved in her own constituency with families dealing with autism, and in particular working with the *Yorkshire Post* on a campaign to target loneliness. Kate recalls her dedication to that cause: 'In amongst everything to do with Syria, she actually spoke and had the time to delve into this issue of loneliness, and how to help older people, and she did it with absolute passion and she was really going away trying to find really practical solutions of how to help people in Yorkshire: how to get to isolated people.' The ideas they came up with together resulted in her setting up a commission – an example, says Kate, of how 'she really bridged the gap between things that matter to her constituency and issues of national importance too'.

As a person? She was 'very warm, very friendly, and actually really funny and quite ready to sit down and have a good natter with you, and it didn't need to be on the hot political issue of the day – although she was extremely informed in everything – but you could have a really personal, quite normal, non-Westminster-bubble conversation with her'. Kate's last memory of her is seeing her talking to someone with 'absolute passion and intensity', wearing a dramatic scarf and swishing it over her shoulder. 'That really sums up how I remember Jo – just seeing her whipping around Parliament and things being done with intense passion.'

For such a dedicated MP, perhaps it is worth giving the last word to one of her constituents, who describes what was lost with her murder, what it was that made her different as a politician: 'She were a people person, she were for us, she weren't for money, she weren't for power. She were a real woman.'

Postscript:

In November 2016, Thomas Mair, an unemployed gardener with a history of far-right political leanings, was found guilty of Jo Cox's murder. He was sentenced to life with a whole-life term: he will never be eligible for parole.

Beatrice de Cardi

Born 5 June 1914; died 5 July 2016, aged 102

Beatrice de Cardi was a pioneering archaeologist who made many important finds in the Middle East. The historian Michael Wood described her as 'part Miss Marple and part Indiana Jones', although she was never keen on either of those comparisons. She was the daughter of a Corsican count and an American heiress, and for over twenty years she was secretary for the Council of British Archaeology.

Beatrice was most at home in the field, as her fellow archaeologist, Harriet Crawford, recalled when speaking to Matthew Bannister for *Last Word*: 'She was always beautifully dressed, she was very particular about her make-up and her general appearance.' Wherever she was – in a lecture hall or the Balochistan desert – the first impression was an impressive one. And her ladylike appearance didn't hinder her, as she herself explained: 'I wouldn't hesitate to pull my dress up if I had to slide down a bank. I think it was just generally the thing that females didn't do, but I was determined to get to a site willy-nilly.'

Beatrice was inspired to take up archaeology when she attended a lecture by the eminent archaeologist Sir Mortimer Wheeler while she was at UCL studying economics, as Dr Derek Kennet of Durham University recalled. She saw a poster for Sir Mortimer Wheeler's series of lectures on Roman archaeology, and these lectures hooked her on the subject for life. She ended up working for him, and, after her war service in China, he encouraged her to set off on her first intrepid expedition. In spite of a series of bureaucratic jobs, she had a yearning to explore, and 'ended up in Karachi and Lahore just after Partition ... she went out on quite long expeditions into one of the woolliest areas of Pakistan, and Balochistan, which were really quite dangerous'.

As Harriet Crawford notes, it was particularly unusual for a woman to go into these tribal areas: 'She said very firmly that when she was out on her fieldwork she was neither a man nor a woman, she was just a *professional*, and she was treated as such by the people she met.' It was an attitude that led to her garnering a huge amount of respect from the various rulers she encountered.

There was certainly an element of old-fashioned adventure and romance to her travels. Derek Kennet described her travelling around 'on camels and horses with a bunch of tribesmen with her and she had a Beretta in her handbag'. In this way, Beatrice said, 'I found innumerable sites that other archaeologists had just passed by.' She was scrupulous in attributing a lot of her success to the help of a man called Sad Adin – a subordinate official in the Pakistan Archaeologist Department who, in her words 'showed me what to look for. He was illiterate, but I learned really more from him than from any academic course or books that I had read.'

For Derek Kennet, the importance of her work cannot be overstated – the area she was working in, Balochistan, is 'on the fringes of these great Bronze Age developments'. So her work was concerned with a vital subject: gaining an understanding of 'how civilisation was developing, and what these fringe areas were doing and what was happening in them, and how the trade contact between these different areas was going on'. In answering these questions, 'her collection of sites and her ability to date them and understand how settlement was changing and so forth, at this time, is really a fundamental'. He describes her finds as 'like a trail' as she picked up a certain type of Bronze Age grey ware, the incidence of which 'slowly led her down towards the Gulf'.

'Her key contribution was Ras al-Khaimah.' This is one of the smaller and more northern of the emirates, and its archaeology has a lot to tell us about the development of trade and civilisations. In 1968, Beatrice was the first to go out and do a proper archaeological survey there, 'and she found *so* many sites, and she found Bronze Age cultures and she found the later Islamic settlements and so forth, big trading cities like Julfar on the coast, which had been trading in Chinese ceramics and silks and spices and incense of the Indian Ocean and she found those locations'.

In spite of the picturesque side of her reputation, Beatrice herself bridled at the comparison to a swashbuckling archaeologist hero: 'I don't think I resemble Indiana Jones in many ways, and I would prefer not to be compared with him because I have an image to project which I want to be an academic one, not that of an adventurer.'

Nevertheless, she went on into her late nineties, still going on digs. Derek Kennet says they used to joke that she was the world's oldest archaeologist. She herself knew the value of what she could still contribute, admitting that she could no longer get in and out of the trenches to excavate, but knowing that her knowledge and expertise were as sharp as ever in identifying pottery and cataloguing material.

Derek Kennet is almost rueful in summing up the colossal nature of her achievement: 'I ran a museum myself out there and I did a lot of surveying. Sometimes we would go out and we would find an archaeological site, and we would come back very excited, and we would go into the museum and find out there in the records that Beatrice had been there thirty years before. And you couldn't really find anything more in Ras al-Khaimah. She seemed to have covered the entire place!'

Aline Griffith,
Countess of Romanones

Born 22 May 1923; died 11 December 2017, aged ninety-four

Aline, Countess of Romanones was a glamorous socialite, a model, a bestselling author and a wartime spy. She was also a close friend of the Duchess of Windsor. She had been born Aline Griffith in a hamlet on the border between New Jersey and New York, and was working as a model when she was recruited to travel to Spain to spy on the Nazis. After the war she married a Spanish count, who died in 1987.

Later on, she spent much of the year in her apartment in New York, where the novelist Jennifer Egan worked as her secretary. Jennifer spoke to Matthew Bannister for Last Word *and described what the countess was like as a presence: 'She had an interesting mix of qualities: she was very glamorous-looking, she was very beautiful, but she also had a very direct sort of earthy quality to her.' Certainly, the social circles in which she moved reflected her glamour – those of Jackie Onassis, Malcolm Forbes and Donald Trump.*

Aline Griffith had worked during the war for the Office of Strategic Services (the OSS) in Spain, where she arrived in 1944. Her own account of her wartime role was matter-of-fact: 'Everybody seemed to be working on one side or the other and it seemed to me that everybody was a spy, but well, many of them pretended that they were other things.'

Charles Pinck, the president of the OSS Society, elaborated on what this work involved: 'What the Americans, and the British, were trying to do in Spain during the Second World War was to make sure that Spain stayed neutral ... Because it was a neutral country it was a hotbed of espionage: there were spies everywhere.'

By his account, Aline was working for the counter-intelligence branch, the most secret part of the organisation – known as 'X-2'. Her job was to be a code clerk, enciphering and decoding messages sent to and from the agents.

An extract from one of her memoirs gives a taste of what this work involved: 'Sitting at a table in front of a small electrical box, I was trying to concentrate as best I could on learning Morse Code. After that I received lessons in ciphering. We were told code rooms were off limits for everyone except the code clerks in OSS offices abroad, since they handled all messages relayed to and from Washington.'

That was her day job, but, as Charles Pinck explains, 'By night her cover was as a socialite employed by American oil companies, and she used that to gather intelligence from Spanish aristocracy. Her cover as a socialite was perfect for intelligence work, because people figured that the only thing she was interested in was putting on make-up.'

According to her memoirs, there were moments of high drama. Charles Pinck described how 'She wrote that after being abducted – she was leaving a Madrid country club with high-ranking Nazis in 1944 – she shot one of the kidnappers, who eventually turned out to be a double agent, but she was uncertain whether or not she killed him.' Her accounts of these days, written in her books *The Spy Wore Red*, *The Spy Went Dancing* and *The Spy Wore Silk*, contain all the elements of a movie: 'He leaned down to a lower drawer and pulled out a metal container, which he unlocked with a key from her right-hand pocket. He held up a small black pillbox. I didn't need to open it to know what was inside, the lethal L-pill, just a quick bite between the teeth and one was dead on the spot.'

She described these books as 'faction', though some in the intelligence community went further and cast doubt on their veracity. As Jennifer Egan puts it: 'You know real life doesn't conform so well to thriller plots generally – and I think that necessitated some invention on her part, which resulted in a lot of criticism when these books would come out from experts who would say: "Wait a minute, that is totally made up."'

Charles Pinck disagrees: 'I know *Women's Wear Daily* wrote an article critical of them when those books came out, because they looked at her OSS file. Well, I have looked at her OSS file – I've looked at lots of OSS files. They contain very little information of an operational nature, so the fact that this wasn't included in her file I don't think necessarily proves it is not true.' He points to a book called *Sisterhood of Spies* by another OSS veteran, Elizabeth McIntosh, who described Aline like this:

> In her undercover days she was Aline Griffith with the pseudo-nym 'Butch'; her striking looks, personality and intelligence made her a favourite with Spaniards of all social classes. She kept her poise under circumstances likely to spoil a less well-balanced person and gained the respect and liking of a large number of people. Her deductions have been accurate in a large number of cases.

Later in life, when Jennifer Egan worked for her, the countess remained a formidable figure: 'She tended towards anger – she had quite a temper, and so if something was bothering her it was very hard for her not to react right in the moment.' Jennifer laughs when asked whether she was a critical employer: 'Oh my god, absolutely! She was incredibly critical.' In particular she took issue with Jennifer's appearance, deeming it not glamorous enough. She also 'hated my spelling; she told me that my bad spelling was infecting her spelling! I remember specifically working on her book about the Duchess of Windsor, I kept spelling Duchess "Dutchess", then she found herself spelling Duchess the same way and she was *enraged* with me.'

Jennifer describes the dinner parties the countess gave, peopled with luminaries such as Oleg Cassini, the Reagans, Calvin Klein and other designers – 'that sort of Upper East Side chic world'. But she was also very frugal: 'She really did not like to spend money.'

There was one famous incident when she was about to give a dinner party for the Reagans and the building's basement caught fire: 'The building was closed off, there was no electricity, everything was dripping with water, and she absolutely *insisted* that this dinner was going to happen nevertheless, over the protestations of the secret services, the building management. The force of her will was something that I really, really, admired. She did not think: "Oh, I see lots of obstacles." She thought: "*This* is what I am going to do. Make it happen.'"

Clearly, it was a mantra by which she lived her whole life.

Pamela Baker, Lady Coleridge

Born 24 July 1947; died 12 August 2018, aged seventy-one

Lady Coleridge was a nurse and adventurer who took part in challenging expeditions. She was born Pamela Baker, in the shadow of Mount Kilimanjaro in Tanzania where her father was serving as a diplomat. She trained as a nurse in London and then rejoined her parents, who by then had moved to Kinshasa, capital of what was then known as Zaire and is now the Democratic Republic of the Congo.

Pamela's daughter, Vanessa Coleridge, spoke to Matthew Bannister for *Last Word*, and began by explaining that her mother was not one to boast about her adventures: 'She was a very modest woman and it was only with her passing that we have come to realise quite how amazing she was and all the fabulous things that she has done.' And what she had done was remarkable. In 1974 Colonel John Blashford-Snell led a British military expedition to explore the Congo River, considered one of the most dangerous in the world. One of the aims of the expedition was to investigate river blindness. Talking to *Last Word*, Colonel Blashford-Snell explained that the expedition was to start at the source of the Congo and navigate to its end. It was estimated to take three months at least. Pamela had become involved after a conversation between Colonel Blashford-Snell and her father: 'He said, "How would you like someone who speaks Lingala, Swahili and French and is a personal friend of President Mobutu?" So I said: "That sounds absolutely marvellous." And he said: "Well, Pam does all that."'

She was a personal friend of the president, he explained, because she had been his nurse. This 'turned out to be extremely useful. In fact, she was the only person allowed to address him by his first name, Albert.'

In Pamela's childhood, according to Colonel Blashford-Snell, she had been known for being very wild. 'At the age of about seven, living in Tanganyika, she used to walk into her mother's rather formal tea parties on her hands most of the time, waving her feet in the air.' Desperate to instil some discipline, her father sent her to a boarding school in England, the Royal Naval School in Haslemere, known for being strict. 'Pam rebelled, and she hated the school bell which rang repeatedly throughout the day, so she took the bell and hid it in the woods, which caused absolute chaos.' Her next act of rebellion was to dye the water system of the school with blue dye, 'so all the pupils and the laundry turned out a sort of ultramarine colour'.

However, by the time Colonel Blashford-Snell first met her, 'She came across as a rather serious young lady with a qualification in nursing.' Her role on the expedition was to be the colonel's assistant, and also one of the leading nurses. Speaking French and Swahili, she also acted as interpreter. She had been trained as a dental nurse, too, which came in handy on the expedition. 'I remember one day watching her pulling out the tooth of one of my sappers, and she got this chap to sit on a chair, and then she put two chairs either side of him – she was only wearing a bikini at the time – and she stood on these chairs above him and pulled upwards and got his friends at the same time to push his shoulders downwards, and that way she got the tooth out.'

She did have to treat the colonel too on occasion, notably when he got malaria. He had to make a speech through the illness: 'My legs started to shake with the rigor, and Pam, sitting close to me, leaned forward and whispered to me: "Keep still, I am going to inject you." And while I stood there she stuck a hypodermic through my trousers, into my thigh, and injected me with chloroquine.'

The expedition went through some very tough terrain: the river is 2,718 miles long, with four sections of extremely dangerous rapids. Pamela appeared not to be daunted by any of this: 'She was sort of fearless really, I don't think she worried at all. She got through all the rapids and so on quite happily; she was tough as any of the men and she always had a tremendous sense of humour.' It was hard work for her, though, since she had the extra duty of nursing the many casualties of sickness, as well as 'rowing the boats and paddling and hacking through jungle at the same time'.

After the Zaire trip she accompanied Colonel Blashford-Snell on various other expeditions: to South America, where they travelled down rivers on traditional reed boats, and to Burma looking for voles.

Vanessa Coleridge explains that after Pamela married Lord Coleridge they moved to Saudi Arabia, where 'she was definitely a little bit mischievous', being 'particularly famous for her home-brewed wine'. Colonel Blashford-Snell backs this up: 'Pam's wine became legendary, but she overdid it on one occasion and all the corks flew out and she found what she had produced was champagne . . . She used to carry the wine into the desert for picnics by putting it in the windscreen washer container for the car.'

Pamela's husband, Bill Coleridge, was a descendant of the poet Samuel Taylor Coleridge. In 1984, Bill succeeded his father as the 5th Baron Coleridge and the couple moved to a twenty-room residence called the Chanter's House in Devon. Even though she was now Lady Coleridge, Pamela never lost her sense of humour. When her daughter returned from a trip to Belize, she welcomed her home in typically irreverent style: 'She had decorated my bedroom all over in a kind of jungle-style, army netting everywhere and cobwebs and spiders and frogs and lizards and I pulled back the sheets and there was a plastic snake in there.'

Colonel Blashford-Snell was simple in his summing-up: 'She was always at the centre of fun, and I would say with a dynamic personality. In fact she was absolutely magnetic. And the great thing was that she never grew old.'

Alex Timpson

Born 25 April 1946; died 5 January 2016, aged sixty-nine

Alex Timpson fostered ninety children over thirty years. Her philan-
thropic approach also influenced the culture of the Timpson shoe repair
and key-cutting business, run by her husband John: the company is
noted for its benevolent treatment of employees. Alex had three children
of her own, and started fostering when she was told that she could have
no more. Her strong belief in helping those less fortunate than herself
has transmitted itself to her children: her son James is not only the
current chief executive of Timpson's, but also chairman of the Prison
Reform Trust. Her other son, Edward, was the children's minister from
2015 to 2017, and her daughter Victoria is a primary-school teacher.

Alex was brought up in Cheshire and met her future husband, John,
at a local tennis club. He spoke to Matthew Bannister for *Last Word*,
and started by describing what she was like: the opposite of a lady
who lunches, she was more likely to be found in a tracksuit, a child
on each arm. 'She never had a handbag, she kept her money in her
bra … the cash went in on one side and the credit cards on the
other, it was quite simple.' The house was always full of pushchairs
and car seats and baby equipment 'because you never knew quite
when the next children were going to come. You never got much
notice, they would arrive two hours after the phone call came, so
you had to be prepared.'

One of her former foster children, David Harper, gives the view
from the other side of the story. He was the 'longest-serving foster
child', having been part of the family for over ten years. 'Because of
the love that she gave me, everything changed almost straight away.
I went to boarding school, I went to prep school, the same one as

her own children, so I was given the best chance in life.'

John Timpson has memories of the first children to arrive into their care: after going through the vetting and approval required for fostering, there had been a long wait. Several months went by, and they were beginning to think nothing would happen. 'Then I arrived one Friday night to find I had got two more children at home. I think they were five and four, about that age, and they stayed with us for six months; exactly six months, because we were short-term foster carers and that's what you did in those days. On the very day the six months was up they were taken away.'

Alex Timpson's own words give a sense of what a wrench this was: 'They went from me to a children's home. I was told that they were going to a proper home, but they didn't. And I used to go and look through the hedge at these children playing in the garden. Oh it was awful! There were tears pouring down.' She would drive home crying. It gave her a hard lesson in not getting quite so emotionally entangled. 'But I gave everything to it.'

John Timpson remembers some of the different characters they fostered: it was a broad spectrum, usually involving children with difficult backgrounds. 'We were pretty unprepared for it. There was no training in those days for foster carers, and certainly the second pair of kids that came to us, they demonstrated their anger. One – the little boy – smashed I think it was 110 panes of glass in my greenhouse.' Clearly, fostering was not always going to be easy. Their approach changed with experience, he says: 'At first, we thought it was just regular mealtimes and lots of cuddles and so on, but, actually, you started to understand that they needed a bit more than that. You had to build their confidence, so a lot of praise, looking for reasons to say "well done" rather than telling them off.' It was clear that each child would need their own approach, often one quite different to the way in which Alex had raised her own children.

As to how the Timpsons' own children reacted to the influx of new siblings, John is frank: 'I have to say our youngest, Edward, [took it] pretty badly to start with.' Edward Timpson's own memories back this up: 'I remember my mother coming to me and saying: "What do you think about having a baby brother, or a baby sister?" And I thought: "Babies, yeah, I quite like babies, that sounds a good idea." Before I knew it, a couple of boys, who we all remember very well, arrived on our doorstep and one was younger than me, but there wasn't that much difference in the age, and I didn't take too kindly to this, and proceeded to lock myself in my bedroom.'

'In actual fact,' says his father, 'he was probably only away for a few minutes.' And by the time a few years had passed, Edward was 'more than anyone' taking the lead in caring for the children and entertaining them.

David Harper describes a childhood where foster children lived with them, some for years, some only for a couple of days: 'While I was there must have been about twenty-five to thirty foster children coming through ... So I basically had lots and lots of brothers and sisters for a very short space of time.'

Alex had interests outside the children, especially sporting interests. She was a keen racehorse owner, and also a big Man City supporter, says her husband, and the day after her memorial service there was a piece in the Manchester City programme about her, as well as one in the *Racing Post*. She had ten racehorses towards the end, and we can perhaps glean something of her character from the names she gave them: 'I think the most interesting name of all of them is one called "Six-One Away" named after a famous victory of Manchester City, when they visited Old Trafford, playing against Manchester United.'

Timpson's the company is known for its philanthropy, something John Timpson ascribes in part to Alex's nature: 'I learned so much from what she did and watching her do it. The business has taken a lot of Alex's caring personality to great advantage in the way we do things.'

The business takes on ex-prisoners – 10 per cent of the workforce join the company from prison. It takes care to look after its staff, letting them have their birthdays off, or giving them access to holiday homes. This stems from Alex's approach to life, says John, as someone who could be tough but who was always using that toughness to stand up for others. 'She reckoned that for all the children that came our way, her job was to look out, be their advocate, to stand up for them.' This manifested itself once when one of her adopted children was a chorister at Chester Cathedral, and got caught misbehaving in evensong. 'Alex stepped in. And, in fact, it wasn't Oliver who was thrown out of the choir, it was Alex who was thrown out of the cathedral.'

As for domestic life, she was certainly not a domestic goddess, being a particular fan of fish fingers. As a reluctant cook, when the family bought a holiday home on Anglesey 'she very quickly decided that the next thing she needed was to buy the local pub, so she could get some decent food'. In fact that was where John was speaking to *Last Word* from, having consumed an excellent lunch in advance. 'Alex would have been delighted,' he said.

Perhaps the last word on Alex should go to David Harper, as one of the many children whose life was transformed by her care and determination: 'She was just my mum, the best woman I could ever have met in my life.'

Anne Coates

Born 12 December 1925; died 8 May 2018, aged ninety-two

Anne Coates was the editor of some of the most acclaimed films of the last sixty years. She won an Oscar for her work on David Lean's classic, Lawrence of Arabia, *and made significant contributions to* The Elephant Man, Murder on the Orient Express *and* Erin Brockovich, *to name but three.*

Anne's daughter, Emma Burford, is also a film editor. She spoke to Matthew Bannister for *Last Word*, recalling Anne's status in the industry, and immediately conjures her mother's enormous charisma, describing her as a 'a bit of a matriarch. She would hold court, is the best way to say it.' She would be at the premiere of some A-list friend of hers and 'would end up surrounded, always surrounded, by movie stars talking to her'. Her modus operandi was just to find a good place to sit, and 'She literally would hold court, and people would come and sit with her, and swap stories with her, and have their photograph taken with her, where you're thinking: "Yeah, but you're George Clooney."'

Anne herself in a *Front Row* interview from 2016 described the moment when love of film took hold of her: 'I was at boarding school. I didn't go to the cinema very much, but they decided to let us go and see one of the more classical films, and one of them was *Wuthering Heights* and I was reading the book at school which was *really* boring, and I went to see the film and the whole thing came alive for me.'

Anne was born in Reigate, Surrey, the daughter of an architect and his wife who was a relative of the British movie mogul J. Arthur Rank. But, as Danny Leigh, curator of the British Film Institute, explained, this wasn't necessarily an asset to Anne's career. Because there was no framework for women to work in the film industry, people thought that being J. Arthur Rank's relation must have worked for her in some way. 'In fact it was exactly the opposite. J. Arthur Rank was a very religious man and specifically didn't want his niece to be involved in the film industry. So she had to overcome all of that to get into the film industry in the first place.' In his opinion, the level of determination she needed to get into the edit room at all manifested in her work 'because you see someone who is utterly confident in their own skill'.

Danny Leigh describes the *Lawrence of Arabia* shot which, for him, encapsulates her talent, the iconic shot that she match-cut, 'where you suddenly move from a lighted match, when Lawrence is simply a civil servant, to the sunrise in the desert, when for the first time, we are about to meet Lawrence of Arabia'. This was the shot that Steven Spielberg referred to as the moment that inspired his love for film, but 'it wasn't a shot, it was a piece of editing'.

Anne herself described how this cut came about: 'David Lean said: "Well, it's nearly perfect," but he said just go and take it away and finesse it. I literally took two frames off the outgoing shot, I think. And I brought it back and David said, "That's great," and that's how it is today.'

The Elephant Man is another great work of hers. Emma Burford remembers playing a part in her mother's involvement – it was she who read the script, which brought her to tears, and persuaded her mother into it. Anne was concerned about how the film would convey the character: 'She said: "I'm really worried that [the director] is going to make it into a freak show." And I said, yes, but that's why you have to do it, because if you are editing it then you will stop him from doing that.'

Danny Leigh explains what makes Anne's work on this film so powerful: the contrast between the 'moments in that film which were frenzied and panicky', such as when John Merrick is being pursued by a crowd when he arrives in London – 'it is this incredibly adrenalised moment and there is a lot of editing going on, a lot of physical editing going on' – and the serene calmer moments, such as the scenes set in the London Hospital, 'where she knew to just let the scene unfold and not do anything. That was the genius of her editing: knowing when to essentially apply her foot to the pedal and when to take it off again.'

For Anne herself, editing was a creative job, one whereby you could improve an actor's performance and enhance the film

Sex scenes did not dismay her, according to Danny Leigh – a good thing, since one of her last films was *Fifty Shades of Grey*. 'Anyone who sees pictures of Anne Coates sees this incredibly grand maternal figure: she is beyond cuddly; she is not the person you would immediately associate with *Fifty Shades of Grey*. Yet, in fact, clearly nothing that was going on in that film fazed her in the slightest.' Actually, she felt that the film could have been 'more raunchy'.

Emma Burford described her mother as being 'extremely competitive, right up until the end, and that included with me'. In her last years, Anne moved into the Motion Picture and Television Fund assisted living campus. Given that the place was full of film people, she lived 'like a queen. It was fantastic, she was holding court at every dinner.' One day when Emma was visiting her for lunch, 'She looked over my shoulder at a woman and she went: "Emma, Emma, look over there!" And so I looked over, and there was a very elderly lady with an oxygen tank attached to her, and she went: "She's our competition." And I went: "What?" And she went: "She's our competition, she's also an editor." This is my mother at ninety-two – still looking at the competition.'

In 2007 she was presented with a BAFTA fellowship. In her acceptance speech she paid tribute to the job which she loved, one that, as she put it, paid her to look into the eyes of some of the most handsome men in the world.

Clearly, a woman who had spent her life doing what she loved.

Hilary Lister

Born 3 March 1972; died 18 August 2018, aged forty-six

Hilary Lister defied a progressive illness to become the first disabled woman to sail solo around Britain. She did so while paralysed from the neck down, steering and controlling her yacht by blowing and sucking through plastic straws. Her achievements prompted the sport's governing body to declare her one of the top four sailors in the world.

Hilary's mother, Pauline Rudd, spoke to Julian Worricker for *Last Word*, and talked first of all about Hilary's childhood: 'She always called herself the third of four boys, so that probably tells you everything. The boys would use her as a goalpost before she could walk.' It was a rough-and-tumble childhood and she loved to be active.

It wasn't until her teenage years that illness struck: when she was around thirteen she suddenly rang up her mother from the train station and asked to be picked up because she couldn't walk. Hilary's sudden immobility meant she used a wheelchair from the age of fifteen, gradually losing the use of all of her body from the neck down. She was eventually diagnosed with a degenerative condition: Reflex Sympathetic Dystrophy. 'For me,' says her mother, 'the pain was, just at the moment when her life should have been opening out, it suddenly closed in. But she was absolutely determined that it wasn't going to stop her.'

She got into sailing when her health began to deteriorate sharply; having gone to Oxford, she started a PhD at Canterbury. However, it was then that she lost the use of her arms. 'And, of course, if you think about it for a minute, that changes your entire life because you can't sit up in bed, you can't pick up a cup, you can't wash yourself.

It's much more limiting than just being in a wheelchair.' Not surprisingly, she became very depressed, almost unable to see the point of living, and it was at this moment that an acquaintance suggested that Westbere Sailing Club had facilities for disabled sailors. Her mother describes the change in her as 'almost miraculous. They put a garden chair on a sailing dinghy, taped her to it, literally, with duct tape, and then they started sailing. They say she had been on the water thirty seconds and she was just so excited.' It was only a few weeks later that she announced that she wanted to sail the Channel. The person who ran the sailing club said, 'Well, yes, I am sure we can fix up to sail across there. And she said: "No, no, you don't understand, *I* want to sail – on my own – across the Channel."

That this was possible was down to the boat mechanic at the club, who looked at the way her wheelchair worked – on a blow-sip mechanism – and realised they could adapt something similar for the boat. The sip-puff method basically meant that she had a straw in her mouth, explains Pauline: 'At first two straws, so just one for the sails and one for the rudder, but then later they brought a third one in which controlled the keel and the GPS system.'

What did this new development mean to Hilary? In her own words: 'It's freedom, it is me alive. It is just one wave at a time really. Where the wind's coming from, are my sails set right? I am talking about being independent in my life and that's something that is new, completely new.'

Her mother describes how in sailing she found a way to leave the difficulties of her life behind: 'I suspected sometimes she just would like to stay longer on the sea and not come back to all the limitations of the land.'

In 2005 Hilary became the first quadriplegic to sail across the English Channel solo. The following year she mirrored the achievement by becoming the first female quadriplegic to sail around the Isle of Wight alone. She won the *Sunday Times* Helen Rollason Award for Inspiration in 2005, and in 2009 became the first disabled woman to sail solo around Britain.

Hilary's was a progressive condition. She knew what lay ahead at some point, a difficult thing for herself and for her family, though given the rarity of her condition, says her mother, it was perhaps a good thing that they couldn't see the future clearly. 'In a way we didn't know and perhaps that's another blessing. . .She didn't know quite how the disease would progress, 'but she did feel that life was very urgent. So, if you look at what she crammed into her years – I mean most able-bodied people would find it difficult to do it in 146 years, I should think, not in forty-six.'

Sailing had given her back some of the life she had lost. For Hilary, 'The boat is where I am me, so I am alive. It's my place. It's bizarre for someone who spends such a lot of time on their own to want to be alone. But it's a different sort of peace.'

Valerie Pettit

Born 13 June 1929; died 28 December 2019, aged ninety

Valerie Pettit would not necessarily have appreciated being featured on the radio, or in a book. She was the hugely discreet senior MI6 operative who led one of the UK's most daring exfiltration operations, getting the double agent Oleg Gordievsky out of Russia when his cover was blown.

Valerie was born near Lord's cricket ground in London, the daughter of a solicitor and his Scottish dancer wife. She went to boarding school and read English at Exeter University before joining the Foreign Office. After a brief spell as a secretary, her talents were recognised and she was transferred to MI6, where she quickly rose through the ranks. After her retirement she was given permission to tell her story to the journalist Ben Macintyre on condition of anonymity.

He describes her as 'charming, grey-haired, very polite, extremely traditional . . . you know we sat down to tea and bone china at exactly 4.10. There were four squares of perfectly aligned biscuit. She was . . . very old-fashioned in lots of ways.' She was also 'highly intelligent', 'very punctilious, very organised, and she didn't suffer fools gladly. She didn't take any nonsense, particularly from men.' Most of all, she was 'ferociously discreet. She was one of those people who found it very difficult to tell her secrets, although after a while she loved telling her secrets.'

Valerie's career sounds just like something out of John le Carré's *Tinker Tailor Soldier Spy*. She served in different MI6 stations around the world, including Warsaw, Baghdad, Oman, Mexico City and Prague. By 1978 she was back in the UK, working as deputy to the head of the P5 section that ran Soviet agents and operations.

This is how she got involved in her most challenging assignment, involving Oleg Gordievsky, a highly valuable double agent.

Gordievsky was a KGB officer, Ben explains: 'Nominally he was a diplomat. In reality he was running a large intelligence network in Copenhagen.' But disillusionment was beginning to set in, especially after the crushing of the Prague Spring in 1968. It was around then that MI6, together with the Danish intelligence services, began to put out feelers to recruit him.

As a double agent, he was taking a great risk with his own safety, and it was necessary to have a plan to get him out if necessary. It was Valerie who came up with this plan, one that by its nature had to be groundbreaking: 'No one had ever been exfiltrated from inside Russia before, and you have to bear in mind that this was a society under permanent KGB surveillance with the most heavily defended borders in the world.' The plan became known as Operation Pimlico.

It bore the hallmarks of someone with a 'wonderful imagination'. The plan was this: 'If Gordievsky was seen holding a red Safeway bag from the supermarket on the corner of a particular street in Moscow at 7.30 on a Tuesday evening, that meant he was in trouble and he needed to get out.' As a response, the MI6 officer on duty would then walk past him eating a Mars bar. 'Once the signal had been flown and acknowledged with the Mars bar, Gordievsky would have to get himself to a special rendezvous site south of the Finnish border,' where two MI6 cars with diplomatic number plates would meet him at a predestined spot. They would then 'bundle him into the boot of the car, wrap him in a heat-reflective blanket in the hope that the infrared cameras wouldn't pick him up at the border, and then try and smuggle him across into Finland'.

It was a pretty audacious scheme, and, says Ben, 'there were many within MI6 who thought the plan was completely bonkers'. Finally, though, the signal came through – Gordievsky did stand there with the Safeway bag, and the operation was triggered. 'Amazingly, it went according to plan.' In a final touch, once they had cleared the border and got through, the officer who was driving put on Sibelius's *Finlandia* as loud as possible, so that Gordievsky would hear it from the boot and know that he was safe. 'And when they popped the boot the first person that Oleg saw when he clambered out was Valerie, and it was an extraordinarily touching moment according to everyone who was there. The first thing he said to Valerie was "I was betrayed." He then, in a very Russian gesture, took both of her hands in his hands and kissed them. He regarded her, really, as his saviour.'

It took a while for Valerie to be willing to tell the story. 'Initially she was quite suspicious, but she was in the end extremely open about it and her memory was extraordinary . . . she could remember in absolutely perfect detail.'

After she retired, she retreated into 'complete anonymity, which is of course the tradition of the service'. She went to live with her sister in a village called West Clandon in Surrey, and nobody there knew anything about what she had done. 'As far as anybody knew she was just a lovely, polite, quiet little old lady who enjoyed going to the opera and taking walks in the country.' Everything about her spoke of an old-fashioned kind of discretion, even when she was finally allowed to tell her secrets. It was, says Ben, 'really most impressive . . . and quite hard to find these days . . . someone who had achieved something quite as remarkable as this but was really quite happy not to tell anyone'.

As for the fact that she was being discussed on the radio? 'I think she would have claimed to be very cross about it; in fact I think she'd be secretly rather delighted.'

Marita Lorenz

Born 18 August 1939; died 31 August 2019, aged eighty

Marita Lorenz's life was truly extraordinary and, unsurprisingly, inspired a television film, My Little Assassin. *At various points she had an affair with Fidel Castro, she plotted alongside a group of Cuban exiles led by Frank Sturgis (who was later convicted as one of the Watergate burglars), she gave evidence to a congressional committee about the assassination of John F. Kennedy, and she had a daughter with a former dictator of Venezuela. And all that after a remarkable childhood. Born in Germany in 1939, she ended up in Bergen–Belsen at the age of five because of the alleged spying activities of her mother.*

The writer and commentator Michael Carlson explained that, as the youngest of her parents' four children, Marita was brought along with her mother when she was taken and was therefore in the children's nursery at the camp. After the war ended, her mother started working for the Americans. It was at this point that the defining moment of Marita's life occurred: 'Marita was raped at the age of seven by an American serviceman and testified at his trial . . . and you can take a lot of the insecurities that follow from that.'

By the time she was a teenager, the family had moved to New York. Her father was working as the captain of a cruise ship, and she 'somehow persuaded her parents to take her out of school and let her work on the ship'. She was a nineteen-year-old girl, without much education, when the ship made a visit to Havana. It was 1959, and the Cuban revolution had just taken place.

It is hard to separate the facts from fiction, but, says Michael Carlson, 'In whichever story you believe, she meets Fidel Castro, who comes on board with his twenty-four bearded assistants and at some point takes a fancy to her.' She was very beautiful, in the style of Priscilla Presley. According to one story, at this point 'Castro kisses her in her room.' She herself would refer to this moment as an 'infatuation' at first sight. Things moved very quickly: Marita by her own account went back to New York on the ship, and Castro almost immediately sent a plane for her to join him in Havana. What she had thought would be a couple of weeks turned into more than eight months, and she became pregnant by him.

It was at this point, Michael Carlson says, that she met Frank Fiorini, who would later be called Frank Sturgis. He would play a major part in her life from then on. He was 'someone who has worked for gangsters, has worked for American intelligence, was with Castro coming out of the mountains and so is trusted by Castro. And he tells her that he can get her out of Havana.' This was necessary because she had lost her baby at seven months in mysterious circumstances. She left Havana and moved to Florida, and it was there that 'she basically is persuaded that she should kill Castro'.

According to her, the CIA asked her to kill Castro because 'they said we don't like his uniform, we don't like his beard, we think he's turning communist, would you do this country a great deed and kill him?'

Michael Carlson picks up the story: 'They gave her a couple of pills to put into Castro's food or drink.' But, in a mistake that seems almost farcical, she put the pills into a jar of cold cream, and 'when she gets to the hotel she realises that the pills have sort of dissolved into the cold cream'. The plan thwarted, she returned to Miami where she joined the anti-Castro Cubans, whose circles included Frank Sturgis. 'And this is where it gets really interesting, because she starts meeting a lot of the key players that we find in the murky world of the Kennedy assassination.'

According to interviews with Marita in later life, she questioned Sturgis as to whether he had had anything to do with the assassination. 'He said, "Oh who gives a shit, who is going to prove it?" He said, "We kill a lot of people, what the hell's the difference?"'

While working as a courier for Sturgis and his colleagues, she met the former dictator of Venezuela, Marcos Pérez Jiménez, who had been exiled from his country and was living in the USA. He was also involved with Sturgis through the International Anti-Communist Brigade, which was an operation backed by the CIA. Marita 'becomes his mistress, and she has a child by him, a daughter named Monica'.

Michael Carlson points out that it is hard to extricate the truth from the lies in much of what went on at this time. However, there was an incident when she flew to Venezuela to see Jiménez, who by that point was in prison there. 'According to her the Venezuelans who brought her there put her in jail in a cell next to him with no window or anything, and then took her away and left her in a deserted village on the Brazilian border in the middle of the Amazon rainforest where she spent five or six months before she could get back.' This sounds too fantastical to be true, but John Stockwell, an ex-CIA agent who wrote a book called *In Search of Enemies*, looked into this story, says Michael Carlson, 'and it turned out to be true, it was easy to verify'. As he puts it, if you look at all the stories she told about her life, 'there's always a kernel of truth . . . but not always the whole truth'.

Pioneers and Innovators

Most of the *Last Word* subjects were born in the early or middle part of the twentieth century, coming of age at a time when women weren't expected to become forensic scientists, or vicars, or outstanding athletes. Some of these women – like Nobel Prize winners Elinor Ostrom or Wangari Maathai – had their achievements recognised. However, many of them have been less well sung, overlooked because of their gender. These are the people who helped change that. Clever, strong, ingenious and creative, they each took a step that moved the world forward.

What they tend to share is a quality of resourcefulness – and not just those of them who were actually inventors (though certainly Valerie Hunter Gordon saw an opportunity every time she was faced with a chore). We see it in Janet Rowley, finding a space to do pioneering cancer research at the kitchen table; in Jerrie Mock, rigging her standard-issue plane so she could fly around the world; in Rita Levi-Montalcini, gathering eggs from local farmers for her experiments before thriftily turning them into supper. And all these women achieved what they did by doing what they loved: in following their dreams they changed the road for the people coming up behind them. Perhaps Janet Rowley put it best: 'What are the questions that excite you? Those are the things you should do.'

These are women who forged a path: women who didn't accept the status quo.

Wangari Maathai

Born 1 April 1940; died 25 September 2011, aged seventy-one

Wangari Maathai was the first African woman to win the Nobel Peace Prize. The 2004 award recognised her campaigning work for human rights and the environment. In an interview the day after receiving the prize, Wangari caused controversy when she appeared to suggest that Aids was deliberately spread by the West to wipe out black people. She later insisted that this was not her view.

Wangari had been a pioneer for most of her life. Born in a small village in Kenya, she avoided the Mau Mau rebellion because she had been sent away to a boarding school run by Italian nuns. Her education in her native country, and then in the USA and Germany, led to her becoming the first woman in post-independence Kenya to take a PhD and the first woman to run a university department there. She founded the Green Belt movement, dedicated to encouraging the planting of trees. One of her colleagues in the movement, Kamoji Wachiira, spoke to Matthew Bannister for *Last Word*, describing her as a 'visionary', particularly with regard to the way she focused on the role of rural women and their place in society.

Wangari herself was very clear about what the important issues for women were – drinking water, food and firewood. 'And so I thought: why not plant a tree? Because if you plant a tree you will get income, because you can sell wood.' This was the start of a campaigning life that would become more difficult and controversial as the years went on. As Kamoji Wachiira explains: 'It wouldn't have been controversial if she had stayed simply planting trees,' but her work developed from there, so that by the early 1980s she was involved in community organisation, in particular encouraging women to stand up for their rights. 'And the system, the establishment, thought: "She has overstepped, the women are overstepping, they are not supposed to be organising, they are supposed to act individually."'

This led to various repercussions in her life, he says: pressure was put on the women and on Wangari in particular, she was hounded by the authorities, fired from the university. Her reaction spoke of her character, her basic response being, 'If you challenge me, it will just encourage me more to be more committed.'

In 1992, Wangari and the mothers of political prisoners staged a hunger strike in a corner of a park in the centre of Nairobi. After four days the protesters were forcibly removed by the police. Wangari and three others were knocked unconscious and had to be taken to hospital. According to Kamoji Wachiira, this only strengthened her. Each incident 'of her groups being beaten, arrested, detained without charge, jailed for days, increased her determination, and their determination, the other women'.

One of the prisoners they were campaigning for was Kang'ethe Mungai. Speaking to the programme on the phone from Kenya, he remembers his first meeting with Wangari in 1992, when he was liberated from prison and she greeted him with a hug, saying 'Welcome to freedom.' He is emphatic about her significance to him – he owes her his life, he says; she is his 'second mum'.

In 2004, when the news came through that she had won the Nobel Peace Prize, she was caught completely unawares. 'She was in the dust somewhere,' says Kamoji Wachira, when a helicopter arrived, blowing the dust up in its wake, and telling her to answer the telephone. According to her own account, Wangari had no inkling that she was going to get the award and she found some poetry in the fact that she was in view of Mount Kenya at the time. 'It's one of the most beautiful creations, it juts out, and for generations this mountain was a spiritual inspiration. And so as I reflected on the prize that I had been given, I watched that mountain and I knew that I was trying to save it from destruction. And I actually felt like it was smiling at me, but also at the same time urging me on.'

The former president of Ireland, Mary Robinson, is now an environmental campaigner herself. She says she was initially surprised when Wangari won the Nobel Peace Prize, because she didn't think it would be awarded to someone who focused on the environment and women's leadership. But of course she realised immediately 'that this was an entirely appropriate message, particularly for the twenty-first century. Because since then, and influenced by Wangari Maathai, I have moved in that direction.' Mary has established an Irish foundation for climate justice, one that 'links human rights, development and the negative impact on the poorest of climate change. But it was Wangari who had insights into that, long before, and who was opening up the space for many of us to make the connection.'

Wangari was, it seems, somebody of great courage, and also somebody whom others would be prepared to follow. Kamoji Wachiira puts this down to her being 'very charismatic – you couldn't resist her smile – and very empathetic'. Mary Robinson gives a sense of her passion and commitment, describing how she would, when speaking at the UN, become so passionate that she would get warned for carrying on past the allotted two minutes. 'I always loved the fact that she wasn't intimidated by flashing lights. We would meet afterwards, and laugh, and embrace, and she would say to me: "I broke the rules again, Mary."' She recalls speaking on a panel with Wangari in Germany, addressing young German people. 'I was standing on a platform beside Wangari, and the moderator was more or less bringing things to a close ... and somehow the moment wasn't right to end the whole thing, they were still waiting for something. And Wangari walked further out on to the front of that platform and began to sing, and she sang the sort of songs that the young could join in, some of the gospel songs, some of them songs that had good choruses, and the place just went electric.'

Kamoji Wachira points to the complex position that Wangari held in her native country. Internationally she was lauded, and won many awards including the Nobel. Yet she did all this while facing a certain amount of opposition: 'She was not a darling of the Kenyan establishment. Outside Kenya she was a star, but in her own country ... she was not much of a prophet.'

Elinor Ostrom

Born 7 August 1933; died 12 June 2012, aged seventy-eight

Professor Elinor Ostrom won the Nobel Prize in Economic Sciences for her work on the management of commonly owned resources, such as forests or the ocean. Her theories affected policy on climate change, fisheries and the supply of water, and are now even being applied to outer space. Professor Ostrom, the only woman to win the prize, was a political scientist by background.

Elinor founded the Workshop in Political Theory and Policy Analysis at Indiana University with her husband Vincent, to encourage collaboration across different academic disciplines. For *Last Word*, Matthew Bannister spoke to one of her colleagues there, Dr Daniel Cole, who described the basis of her work and how it was a response to a theory dating from the 1960s called 'tragedy of the commons'. This theorised that any resources that are not owned by individuals, and are instead kept for use and access for many, the so-called common-pool resources, will be overexploited and destroyed unless regulated or privatised. 'For example, a fishery, offshore, in the absence of some management regime, it's open access – anyone can go out and catch as many fish as they like. And so unless we somehow figure out a way to engage in collective action to control overuse of those resources, they will be overexploited and eventually these stocks will be destroyed.' To investigate this, Elinor went out and did fieldwork and analysed empirical studies, 'and found that, contrary to this theory of the tragedy of the commons, people did in fact engage in local collective action in order to successfully manage co-owned resources over very long periods of time'.

Dr Jill Stuart of the London School of Economics described how

Elinor went about this work: 'She didn't just sit in an office and pontificate about these things: she went out in the world.' In Los Angeles she looked at groundwater resources. In Indonesia she investigated fishing; in the Swiss Alps she spoke to farmers who pooled their grazing areas. She grounded her theory in real-world examples.

She came to the conclusion that individuals at the grass-roots level could sometimes have an impact where international governance could not. Elinor's emphasis was on how the people on the ground managed their own behaviour: 'We now have over 200 forests that we have studied around the world. One of the *absolutely* key, most important variables, as to whether or not a forest survives, or continues, is whether local people monitor each other, and its use. Not officials – locals.'

The conclusion, Jill Stuart says, is that local solutions are more effective than top-down ones because 'you have to go to the grass-roots level, where people have sentimental attachment to the resources that they are using, and explore how the systems of governance are working at that level, and improve upon them,' something that obviously has a significance in, say, the fight against climate change. This led, as Daniel Cole described it, to Elinor developing 'a set of what she called design principles, for determining or predicting the success or failure of common property regimes'.

As Elinor herself put it: 'What we have ignored is what citizens can do, as opposed to just having somebody in Washington make a rule. How does that get all the way down to management of forests, fisheries, irrigation systems et cetera?'

She was known in academic circles for being 'very interdisciplinary', says Jill Stuart, 'and that was one of the things that I, personally, most respected about her'. It meant she could influence different areas – economics, public policy, politics. She was perhaps even an anthropologist in some ways. 'Academia can be very conservative, people like to pigeonhole their disciplines sometimes. And so in other ways I think it made some people uncomfortable. When she won the Nobel Prize in Economics there was a bit of surprise in some circles, and I think that was due to the fact that she wasn't explicitly an economist.'

Daniel Cole described what she was like in person, a warm, smiling woman who had the ability to make everyone feel good. 'Her presence was much greater than her personal stature: she was about five foot four, somewhat stocky, she sort of resembled somebody's grandmother, but always coming in with great energy and her charisma.' And Jill Stuart echoes this: 'She was very down to earth'; the first time Jill Stuart spoke to her, Elinor had just won the Nobel Prize, 'and I remember that she referred to herself as Lin: there was absolutely no pomp and circumstance'.

Daniel Cole adds an anecdote from the end of Elinor's life, when she was in hospital. When the nurses and doctors came in to explain to her what the situation was, 'they would ask her: "Do you have any questions?" And as soon as they asked that, she would get a twinkle in her eye and she would respond to them, "Oh yes, I have lots of questions. But not about this!"' Even right at the end of her life, she was always thinking about the issues that she was trying to solve. 'That's what she was focused on from the time she got up in the morning until the time she went to bed at night.'

Rita Levi-Montalcini

Born 22 April 1909; died 30 December 2012, aged 103

Professor Rita Levi-Montalcini was the Italian scientist who won the Nobel Prize for her work on cell growth, including the abnormal growth that leads to cancer. She was still carrying out experiments as she reached her 100th birthday.

Much of Rita's career was spent at the University of Washington in St Louis, where she collaborated with biochemist Stanley Cohen, but she divided her life between the USA and her native Italy: she was appointed a life member of the Senate and campaigned there for women's rights. Her friend and colleague Professor Antonino Cattaneo describes her as 'a small, minute, seemingly weak lady' who seemed 'frail' but who 'expressed such a great, great, strength. She always said that the greatest joy that one can have is having ideas and nesting them in your mind.'

Rita Levi-Montalcini was born into a Jewish family in Turin; during the war Jews were banned from taking part in scientific work, so she carried out experiments in secret. When war was declared it became clear that she could not remain and work in Turin, and so the family moved to the countryside, where she 'continued to work, completely ignoring what was happening around me'. According to Professor Cattaneo, 'She set up a small laboratory in her own bedroom at her house.' It was a very basic setup, where she had to make her own scalpels to do the work that she was conducting on dissecting chicken embryos. 'The problem was also to get the eggs because there was a shortage of food in those times. So she would cycle around farms and collect eggs, saying that they were for her children.' Apparently, after the experiments the eggs would then be used for cooking. 'And her brother eventually discovered this, and he would refuse to eat the scrambled eggs that had gone through Rita's experiments.'

In 1986 she was awarded the Nobel Prize in Physiology or Medicine in recognition of her work on cell growth, an achievement she described in her acceptance speech as 'like finding oneself on the top of the highest peak of the Himalayan chain, Everest'. The award was due to the significance of the protein she had discovered, nerve growth factor, or NGF. This is a critical factor in the development of the nervous system, because it guides the growth and health of the nerve cells and nerve fibres. 'Of course,' Professor Cattaneo emphasises, 'this work has groundbreaking importance for applicative and potentially therapeutic purposes.'

She never married or had children of her own. The story she told to explain her decision not to have a family, says Professor Cattaneo, was that, as a young girl, she had once 'liked this hat with red cherries, and her mother wanted to get her this hat'. But her father had forbidden it, and watching this Rita had felt sorry not for herself but for her mother. She loved her father, but she did not want to get married and be told what to do.

She was extremely well known and well loved in Italy. 'When she would go in the streets people would stop her, would cheer her , would shake hands, would give her flowers, she loved flowers a lot.' Tens of thousands of people lined up to honour her at the Senate of the Republic when she lay in state before her funeral. 'I mean,' says Professor Cattaneo, 'we are a republic, but she, if I may say so, she was something like a very, very, popular queen.'

The Rev. Joyce Bennett

Born 22 April 1923; died 11 July 2015, aged ninety-two

Joyce Bennett was the first Englishwoman to be ordained as a priest in the Anglican communion. The ceremony took place in Hong Kong in 1971. (Joyce wasn't the first woman to become an Anglican priest: that distinction fell to the Rev. Florence Li Tim-Oi, who had been ordained amid great controversy, in 1944, also in Hong Kong.)

Joyce Bennett was born in London. She recalled a prescient incident while playing with her brother George as a child, when her parents would go to church and leave the children behind, 'and that was when he began to play at being the vicar, and I was the congregation, and he didn't like my suggestion that 'it's my turn to preach now'. He said: 'Oh no, girls don't do that!'

Joyce was educated at Burlington School, where she was head girl. She took a degree in history and then a diploma in education. For *Last Word*, Matthew Bannister spoke to the BBC's former religious affairs correspondent, Ted Harrison, who gave the background to her ordination: 'She trained as a missionary and went out in 1949 to Hong Kong and began a career as a teacher and she very quickly settled down into Hong Kong life.' She started a school, St Catherine's. She learned Cantonese. When the Anglican Consultative Council, which is the governing body there, decided that it was prepared for a local bishop to ordain a woman, 'almost immediately Bishop Baker of Hong Kong decided that he would ordain Joyce Bennett'.

Matthew also spoke to Christina Rees, a member of the General Synod of the Church of England and a leading campaigner for the ordination of women, asking her how the landmark moment of

Joyce Bennett's ordination was received in the wider communion. 'I think it gave a lot of people a huge amount of hope, and of course was declared scandalous by some.'

Some months after her ordination, Joyce returned to England because her mother had been in an accident. Ted Harrison explains what happened: 'She actually held a Communion service, a private one in a private home with some of her friends, as a thanksgiving for her mother's recovery.' This made it the very first time that the Eucharist had been celebrated by a woman in England. 'Doctor Ramsay, the then Archbishop of Canterbury, when he heard about it, actually said that he appreciated Joyce's motives in holding the service and assured her that her action had been quite proper.'

But when Joyce moved back to the UK permanently, some in the Church were not so accepting of her status, as Christine Rees describes: 'She was given a ministry at St Martin-in-the-Fields, which has a strong Chinese congregation, and because she was fluent in Cantonese she found a natural place there and was able to minister there. But she was *not* able to minister as a priest; she was only able to minister as a deacon.' Ted Harrison takes up the story: 'However, when she had her visiting cards printed, as the minister to the Chinese community, in English she had no mention of her priesthood, but in Chinese she did.'

'Canny Joyce!' says Christina Rees. A very Church of England situation, then, with rather blurred edges. Or as Christina Rees puts it: 'We are talking about Anglican fudge – that's what we call it!'

The Bishop of London, Graham Leonard, was not a supporter, objecting to the ordination of women. 'He expected that, should Joyce be presiding at a Eucharist a man, a male priest, would have to be present,' says Ted Harrison. What happened next hit the headlines: the Movement for the Ordination of Women invited Joyce to celebrate Communion at Church House in Westminster, a move that led to them being banned from using the building. According to Christina Rees: 'She presided at an informal, private, Eucharist, but because it was in Church House – which is the official Church of England headquarters in Westminster – that created a furore and it created this explosion of sharp feelings.' On the one side were people saying: 'Don't be ridiculous: this was private, and anyway this is a woman who was ordained priest just doing what she has been doing for years.' On the other, there were those whose attitude was: 'This must not have happened, and she should be censured.'

Joyce's own view on it was simple: 'In a private capacity, amongst friends, with the public excluded, I see no reason why I should not answer pastoral need.'

Ted Harrison describes Joyce as 'a formidable woman: there was no mistaking that she had been a headmistress'. Florence Li Tim-Oi, her fellow woman cleric, had not had the same attention as Joyce because of complications arising from the political situation in China. When she came into the public consciousness again, the contrast between the two women was striking. They were 'chalk and cheese ... totally contrasting characters. Florence was self-effacing and saintly; Joyce was formidable and the headmistress, and yet the two of them, together, were perfect ambassadors for the possibility – as it only was then – that women could be priests.'

Interestingly, Christina Rees says that Joyce's voice was not strongly heard in the debate that was subsequently to rage on this subject. 'She was not on the General Synod and she was not a major spokesperson, but her presence was definitely felt and resonated in the movement.' She provided a sense of encouragement: 'Of course we can get there, of course we can do this!'

Ted Harrison sees her life as remarkable 'She lived through an entire era of change, way back in the 1960s, when she felt her own call to priesthood and knew it was not legally possible, all the way through to today, when women are being consecrated as bishops all around the world. And her part in that story is a very, very, important one.'

Rosalía Mera

Born 28 January 1944; died 15 August 2013, aged sixty-nine

Rosalía Mera co-founded the world-famous Spanish clothing chain Zara, and became the richest self-made woman in the world. Born in Galicia in 1944 to a working-class family, she left school at the age of eleven to work in a clothes shop. In 1975 she opened the first branch of Zara in Spain with her husband. Over the next thirty years the chain grew into the world's largest fashion retailer, becoming popular because of its quick response to customers' preferences. By the time of her death, the parent company, Inditex, extended to 6,000 stores in eighty-six countries. The reclusive Rosalía retired from the board in 2004, but throughout her life she devoted much of her time and money to charitable foundations.

Journalist Alejandro Zajac spoke to Aasmah Mir for *Last Word*, and started by talking about how Rosalía was regarded in Spain. 'She was well known, but she never wanted to show that much about her private life,' perhaps to shield her children from the press. Fashion journalist Marion Hume echoes this: 'I think as outsiders from Inditex, we know very little about her and that was exactly what they wanted. Zara Inditex is an extraordinarily private company.' As she points out, Rosalía's ex-husband and co-founder is one of the richest men in the world, and yet in comparison to someone like Bill Gates he is extremely low-profile. '[People like that] are very present in our lives. He is not. He has never given an interview, as far as I know she never gave an interview, so we know very little about her.'

One thing we do know, says Alejandro Zajac, is that she considered herself very much to be left-wing. 'She openly supported the

Indignados movement, when demonstrations took place all over the country.' There is of course an interesting dichotomy here, in that she was the world's richest self-made woman and yet still a leftist. It seems an uncomfortable position. 'I don't think she felt uncomfortable at all,' says Alejandro Zajac, 'because her wealth gave her the chance to invest in things she believed [in], and to create a foundation that was very important in her life.' This was the influential Paideia Galiza Foundation, which she formed because her son was born with cerebral palsy.

Marion Hume points out that although Rosalía became one of the most powerful women in Spain, her childhood was very humble. She came from an area, Galicia, that was extremely poor, and – like the rest of Spain at the time – under a dictatorship. Her debut into the world of fashion was 'the most unglamorous entrance ever', via a nightdress factory – 'and we are not talking La Perla, we are talking the things that your aunty might reject'. She and her husband started out as manufacturers, and then opened a shop – originally it was going to be called Zorba, but that was changed to Zara.

Alejandro Zajac explains that what really set Zara apart was its design and production methods, which allowed it to react faster to new trends and to get them from the catwalk into the shops in a matter of weeks. It was of course enormously successful, and by the time of Rosalía's death there were more than 1,700 Zara stores around the world.

Marion Hume explains the appeal of Zara, and what lies behind its success: counter-intuitively, 'perhaps the first thing is there is no Zara style'. In contrast to competitors such as H&M or Topshop, which have a stronger aesthetic that identifies them, 'Zara really is what you want it to be, and I think that's part of its great skill, that it is very fast to adapt to trends.' She gives as an example the white jackets that were once sent to the Manhattan store. When the staff there commented that New York women don't wear white in the city, they only wear cream, keeping white for their holidays in the Hamptons, these jackets were removed overnight and two weeks later, which is *very* fast in a fashion turnaround, the New York stores were full of cream jackets, all of which sold out'.

Asked whether Rosalía Mera was considered a feminist icon, Alejandro Zajac is thoughtful, but thinks not. Overwhelmingly, she was a woman who was proud of where she came from and of her working-class origins, and most of all proud of being a 'self-made woman'.

Janet Rowley

Born 5 April 1925; died 17 December, aged eighty-eight

Professor Janet D. Rowley was a biomedical researcher who demon-strated that cancer is a genetic disease. Her work led directly to the development of life-saving treatment for some leukaemia patients.

Janet Rowley was born in New York City. She studied philosophy and then medicine at the University of Chicago, where she ended up as a distinguished professor of genetics. But she made her break-through while working part-time and raising her four children. Her friend and colleague Dr Francis Collins spoke to Matthew Bannister for *Last Word* and explained what the significance of her contribution was: 'She was one of the first to be able to look at human chromosomes, packets of genetic information, under the microscope, and assess what happens to those in the case of cancer.' Before her work, there was an awareness that cancer was linked to issues with DNA and chromosomes, but that was considered to be an effect of the disease. 'What Janet discovered was, no, quite the reverse, it is a cause: if you have a specific rearrangement of chromosomes, you actually activate a cell to grow when it should not, resulting in a particular type of cancer: in her case, leukaemia.'

Janet's own account of how she moved into this field gives a sense of her character: 'I was a physician, my husband was going to Oxford, I couldn't practise medicine, but I thought: "Well I could learn chromosomes."' She asked a professor at the University of Chicago for access to a microscope and a darkroom. She told him: 'I only want to work part-time because I have three children and, by the way, would he also pay me? And he said yes to all of those conditions.' As Dr Collins puts it, having wheedled her way into the laboratories, 'she would take photographs of chromosomes from cancer cells, and then she would take them home and cut the chromosomes out in little pieces and arrange them to try to figure out what she was looking at, warning her children: "Don't mess with this stuff on the dining table, it might be the future of science!"'

The British geneticist Dr Emily Grossman explains why Janet's work was so important. At that point, it had been identified by other scientists that in patients with chronic myelogenous leukaemia, one of the forty-six chromosomes, chromosome 22, was smaller than it should be. But it wasn't clear why. Janet used a newly developed technique called banding 'to actually look at the picture of the chromosomes under a microscope. And she could see, from this banding pattern, that the small chromosome 22 had actually got the end of it chopped off and it had switched places with the end of chromosome 9. So it is kind of like if you have got two pencils, a red one and a blue one, you break the end off both, and you switch them round.' There had been a genetic switch known as a transloca-tion. 'And this was really crucial, because it was the first time that a genetic basis to cancer had been discovered, or shown. So it meant that the genes from the two chromosomes were in the wrong place, which was what was causing the cancer, and this revolutionised our understanding of cancer as a genetic disease.'

Dr Collins sums up Janet's career: 'It would be exciting enough to be able to say: we now understand the cause of cancer; it's much more exciting to be able to say: we can do something about it.' Janet and her colleagues won the Lasker Prize – an American equivalent of the Nobel – for her work on this chromosome. 'Maybe, had she lived, the Nobel list might have gotten around to recognising her in that regard as well.' Either way, she was considered by her col-leagues and other scientists to be 'in that very, very, stratospheric rank of the most significant contributors to biomedical research of the last century'.

But perhaps it is best to give the last word to Janet Rowley her-self, explaining what it was that drew her to the subject in which she would make such a profound difference: 'I think science should be exciting; most importantly you have to follow your curiosity: what do you find challenging? What are the questions that excite you? And those are the things that you should do.'

Billie Fleming

Born 13 April 1914, died 12 May 2014, aged 100

In 1938, Billie Fleming gave up her job as a typist in London to devote the next twelve months to riding her bike. She ended up setting the world record for the longest distance ever ridden by a woman. As her stepson, Peter Samwell, recalled for Last Word, *Billie's aim was to promote fitness: she had been inspired by a woman called Mary Bagot Stack, who in the 1930s created the Women's League of Health and Beauty. Stack's vision was "a league of women who will renew their energy in themselves and for themselves day by day". And Billie really bought into this concept, and she firmly believed that you could really keep fit just by riding a bike. So she set out to prove it.'*

David Barter, of *Cycling Weekly* magazine, interviewed Billie Fleming on her 100th birthday. She told him how she originally became interested in cycling: 'I couldn't ride a bike, I had never been on a bike before . . . I just met a boy who rode a bike and he introduced me to it.' He explained to Matthew Bannister how unusual Billie's attempt at long distance cycling was: 'There was no world record for women at the time, there was a cycling mileage record that was almost exclusively attacked by men.'

Billie got a bike from the manufacturers Rudge Whitworth, after writing to various bicycle companies saying: 'This is what I am going to do, will you help me, will you support me?' And Rudge apparently came back to her very quickly and said: 'Yes, we are interested, we will give you a bike and some support, we would just like you to go and talk to people at our dealerships as you do your big tour.'

Peter Samwell describes the bike as 'a heavy steel bike. It had three-speed gears. Billie always believed that the modern trend for multiple speed gears was quite unnecessary.' (In her interview with David Barter on her 100th birthday, Billie teased him about his claim to need thirty gears on his bike: 'You don't. You can't tell the difference between them.') By today's standards, Billie's preparations for the challenge were minimal. According to her stepson, 'She didn't carry any water, and she just used cafés and shops to buy a bit of food ... She didn't have the benefits of Lycra, she just wore jacket and shorts, nothing very special at all.'

On the first day of her attempt, 1 January 1938, he says, 'She cycled to Mill Hill and then on to Aylesbury and back to Mill Hill, which is a total of I think about seventy-one miles.' Over the course of the year, her average would be about eighty-one miles a day. Sometimes she clocked up considerably more than that, says Peter Samwell: 'I remember her telling me that she woke up one morning in York and said to herself: I think I will ride home today, and so she cycled all the way back to Mill Hill, 186 miles.' When David Barter asked her how she found this massive ride, her answer was simple: 'I liked it.'

According to David Barter, the cycling press picked up on her record-breaking attempt: 'They covered her mileage on a weekly basis and her progress.' A lovely piece she herself wrote, illustrating a moment on the road, gives an impression of her character as well:

> After having ridden for only two weeks I was slowly climbing a hill, made harder by a strong headwind, when an offside door was flung open in my path; fortunately, I did not swerve but managed to stop against the side of the car to watch a large lorry rumble past where I had been riding. I dismounted and spoke to the car driver and almost immediately received a command from the same 'gentleman' to go to that mythical place of torture.

There was a 'very rigorous' system for checking that she was actually doing the mileage, says David Barter: '*Cycling Magazine* were the custodians of the mileage records, and they demanded that the riders carry with them checking cards, and these checking cards had to be signed throughout the day by witnesses who would verify the location of the rider and the figure on the rider's milometer.'

By the end of the year she had done 29,603.4 miles, which is thirty-five times the distance from Land's End to John o' Groats. According to David Barter, 'She felt fine. She talked about the challenges of the weather and the occasional very, very, steep hill – but she was very fit.' She had set the first world record for the greatest distance cycled in a single year by a woman. And, says Peter Samwell, 'I don't believe that anybody has ever broken that record since.'

As to whether she went on cycling for the rest of her life, the answer is surprising: 'No, because she was married to George Fleming, who was also another famous cyclist; and, once they married, they did a journey from the Atlantic to the Mediterranean, right over all of the mountain passes on the Pyrenees, that was probably the last journey they did. They had other interests, and I guess that life moved on.'

Stephanie Kwolek

Born 31 July 1923; died 18 June 2014, aged ninety

Kevlar – the material best known as the chief component of bulletproof vests – has been credited with saving thousands of lives. It was invented by Stephanie Kwolek, who worked as an industrial chemist at DuPont in Wilmington, Delaware.

For Last Word, *Julian Worricker spoke to David C. Brock from the Chemical Heritage Foundation based in Philadelphia, and started by asking what exactly Kevlar is. 'It's a synthetic fibre . . . a polymer pioneered by DuPont . . . almost like a synthetic steel.' There is a huge breadth of applications in the use of Kevlar, not just in bulletproof vests or in industrial chemistry, but in everyday life. We come across this material, almost unknowingly, all the time: 'It has gone into everything from commercial aircraft, marine transport, ships and boats to your automobile: many brake pads, clutches, gearboxes have parts made with Kevlar in them. Tyres, parts of the aircraft engines, fibre optics – these delicate glass fibres that carry the information are surrounded by multiple layers to make up a fibre-optic cable, one of which is a Kevlar layer.'*

Stephanie described her invention of Kevlar as a case of serendipity. She had persuaded a fellow scientist to spin a carbon-based liquid in the laboratory spinneret and it produced a fibre of unusual stiffness, five times as strong as steel and able to stop a bullet.

Stephanie Kwolek's career was notable not just for this discovery, but for the fact that it was comparatively unusual at that time for women to work in this field at all. David Brock explains that the industry had actually taken a step backwards in equality in the late 1940s and early 1950s. 'There were greater opportunities for women to participate in chemical research and industry during the Second World War. In the post-war [period] their numbers rapidly diminished.' According to Stephanie herself, it was not an easy time to be a woman in the workplace, and many women did not last long in it. She ascribed her own longevity in the field to stubbornness.

The Kevlar discovery has made enormous amounts of money for DuPont – several billion dollars, perhaps. Of course, Stephanie did not directly benefit from that, except, as David Brock points out, 'to the extent that she advanced in her career at DuPont, and received a lot of recognition.' It was not an unusual arrangement for scientists who worked in research in corporate settings, and she did win various awards for engineering.

The chief executive at DuPont described Stephanie Kwolek as 'a true pioneer for women in science'. David Brock gives the reasons why he would agree: 'Her tenacity, her persistence in her research, her role subsequently tutoring and mentoring women and girls to encourage them to participate in the chemical sciences and technology, in chemical engineering, does make her a pioneer.'

The last word in this case goes to Stephanie herself: 'What I love about my work is that I have the opportunity to be creative every day. I love the excitement ... When I reflect back upon my career, I am inspired by the fact that I was able to do something that was of benefit to mankind.'

Lorna Wing

Born 7 October 1928; died 6 June 2014, aged eighty-five

Dr Lorna Wing was the psychiatrist who defined the concept of the autism spectrum. The mother of an autistic daughter herself, she also coined the term Asperger's syndrome, to refer to autistic children who don't have learning disabilities.

Lorna was born in Gillingham, Kent and trained as a doctor at University College Hospital in London. That was where she met her future husband, John Wing, when they were both allocated the same corpse for dissection. The couple both went on to work as psychiatrists at the Maudsley Hospital in South London. She wrote a number of influential books on autism and founded the Centre for Social and Communication Disorders which now carries her name. In 1994 she received the OBE. The director of the National Autistic Society, Carol Povey, spoke to Matthew Bannister for *Last Word* and described Lorna's own connection with the condition. Her daughter 'had quite severe autism, and she recognised when Susie was very young that Susie was behaving in a way that was very different, and interacting with people and the world around her in a way that was very different from other children'. Both Lorna and her husband were psychiatrists, and Lorna focused her research on the condition, 'not only to understand more about Susie, but actually to really understand about autism'. In Lorna's own words, 'You can't treat autism at the moment: no one knows of a medical treatment. But what you can do is to give the children the sort of education that will help to minimise their handicaps and to maximise the skills that they do have.'

Matthew Bannister also spoke to Robyn Stewart, who has

Asperger's syndrome and works to help others understand it. She explains the effect that the syndrome had on her early life: 'I had got into trouble with being bullied and I was really quite angry about it. I knew that I was autistic, but I really didn't know a lot about it. So I started to read about the autism spectrum.'

In particular, her reading took her to the concept of the 'triad of impairments'. This, Robyn explains, 'was a concept really that Lorna Wing and Judith Gould wrote about in their 1979 scientific paper, the Camberwell Study' – so called because they studied people in the London borough of Camberwell over a period of many years. The triad of impairments, as laid down in this paper, are communication, interaction and imagination. However, a note of caution is needed here – this does not mean an impairment of 'creative imagination – there are many people on the autistic spectrum who are very creative'. To draw a distinction, they used the word 'social' as a modifier – 'social communication, social interaction and social imagination'. As Robyn explains, 'What we are actually talking about when we talk about social imagination is things like being able to put yourself in someone else's shoes, seeing someone else's perspective, or being able to understand someone else's intentions.'

Carol Povey describes the other large contribution that Dr Wing made to the understanding of autism: 'One of the other key things that she did was introduce the concept of Asperger's syndrome into the English-speaking world.' This was to illuminate the fact that there are many people who are on the spectrum but do not have severe learning difficulties: prior to this the assumption was that they went together. Lorna 'saw many of the gifts and talents that autistic people were able to bring to their lives, and to the lives of others, such as attention to detail, a real focus on truth, and a very straightforward way of seeing the world'.

Robyn Stewart's description of what Lorna meant to her shows the human significance of her work: 'Lorna was an incredibly amazing person. I feel so privileged to have met her, it is like meeting Paul McCartney, or Elton John ... [she was] a really big, important person and hugely influential in my own life, because I *hated* being autistic, I felt horrible, because I felt I was different and like it was this really bad thing. From learning about what she did, I learned about myself.'

When asked about what Lorna looked like, Robyn's answer is surprising: 'Goodness, do you know what, that's a really good question to ask me, because I have a condition, along with autism, called prosopagnosia ... sometimes it is called "face blindness": I can see faces but I just don't remember them. So I don't really know what Lorna looked like, but she had a really kind voice.'

Carol Povey describes her as 'an amazingly modest and humble person for someone with such a massive intellect. She was small, and she was quite ordinary-looking, but always with a smile on her face.'

What made her so special, according to Robyn, was that 'she loved and accepted people on the spectrum as a whole, she really learned about people and I think that's so important, because everybody on the autistic spectrum is different and the needs of people are so wide'. Lorna knew that the spectrum encompassed people who needed twenty-four-hour care, but also people like Robyn who 'go out in the world, get jobs, live on their own, have partners, have children'. Lorna understood that they too needed help.

It is Carol Povey who sums up Lorna's achievement and her legacy, the pride she would have taken in the fact that people with autism and their families are more able to access 'the services, the support and the understanding that they need to help them to live valued, fulfilling lives'.

Jerrie Mock

Born 22 November 1925; died 30 September 2014, aged eighty-eight

Jerrie Mock was the first woman to fly solo round the world. Known in the media as 'the flying housewife', Jerrie set off in her single-engine plane from Columbus, Ohio on 19 March 1964. She returned twenty-nine days later, having covered 23,000 miles and taken twenty-one stopovers.

Jerrie's sister Susan Reid spoke to Matthew Bannister for *Last Word*, and says flying ran in the family, not least because they traced themselves back to the Wright brothers on her mother's side. At seven, Jerrie was given a ride in a Ford Trimotor plane, and her reaction was immediate: 'When the plane landed, she told my parents: "I am going to be a pilot!"' Jerrie's own voice as she described this, recorded many years later, still carries the excitement of that moment: 'I looked down at the houses and the little tiny cars and I made up my mind I wanted to do that some more.'

Dorothy Cochrane of the US National Air and Space Museum says Jerrie never lost sight of that ambition: 'She took aeronautical engineering as a subject, she went to college, got married, had children, as was the norm in the 1950s, but then she decided to get her pilot's licence after her husband had, and they just started flying around as general aviation pilots.'

The idea of flying around the world arose out of conversations she had with her husband. When she spoke about where she wanted to go, he asked her: 'Well, why don't you just fly around the world?' And she said: 'Well all right, I think I will.' According to Jerrie, her mother didn't want her to go, considering that it wasn't 'ladylike' to

fly. For the rest of her family, the potential worry of such a dangerous undertaking was offset by their knowledge of her character. As
her sister puts it, 'We had so much confidence in her: we knew she
was going to do it.'

She became the first woman to circle the globe alone and the
first woman to fly the Pacific, west to east, solo. The plane itself was
a 'very generic general aviation aircraft, a Cessna 180,' says Dorothy
Cochrane, who describes it as 'a strong and sturdy little single-
engine plane, nothing sophisticated about it, but very rugged and
very reliable'. Jerrie's husband was a co-owner of this plane and they
decided to rig it out, adding extra fuel tanks and making it feasible
to fly round the world.

'Many things went wrong along the way,' says Dorothy Cochrane,
starting with the discovery in the first hours of the trip that her
long-distance high-frequency radio was not working. That necessitated a decision about whether to turn back and fix it, or just carry
on to Bermuda. Deciding to carry on, 'she actually flew out across
the Atlantic Ocean to find small little Bermuda'. It was just one
example of her courage and determination.

After a month, Jerrie arrived back in Ohio to what the news
reports described as 'a heroine's welcome'. Thousands of people
gathered to watch her return, and she received an FAA Exceptional Service medal from President Johnson. When she got off the
plane, exhausted, says her sister, she was greeted by a welcoming
committee that included the mayor and also some of her erstwhile
classmates. Some of them had laughed when as a child she said
she would fly round the world, 'but four of them were there at the
airport with a big sign that said: "Welcome Home Jerrie!"'

Amelia Earhart, because of her disappearance, has become a
legendary name, but Jerrie Mock is not so well known – perhaps,
says Dorothy Cochrane, because Amelia Earhart made a career of
aviation. Jerrie, on the other hand, 'was a self-described housewife
who just wanted to see the world'.

Asked whether she was very proud of her sister, Susan is emphatic: 'Oh, I was. And I am.'

Claudia Alexander

Born 30 May 1959; died 11 July 2015, aged fifty-six

Claudia Alexander was a NASA space scientist who played prominent roles in two missions. She was the last project manager on the Galileo mission to Jupiter and represented NASA on the international Rosetta mission to land the Philae *probe on a comet.*

Claudia was brought up in California. According to Dr Maggie Aderin-Pocock, who presents the BBC's *Sky at Night* programme, 'At first, she didn't want to go into science at all. Her parents said that she should go into engineering, but she actually wanted to go into journalism. So she didn't have stars in her eyes straight away.' But during an engineering internship at NASA, Claudia kept sneaking over to the space building, and her future course was set. She took a master's degree and a doctorate, and then landed a job back at NASA. Her friend and colleague Nagin Cox, speaking to Matthew Bannister for *Last Word*, says that Claudia's role on the Galileo mission expanded as the project developed: 'She started out as a scientist on one of the instruments, and then her long-term dedication to the project ended up with her finishing her time on Galileo as the final project manager.'

Dr Aderin-Pocock described what that project manager role entails: 'Effectively, you are managing, coordinating, making sure that all the requirements of the project are fulfilled.' One feature of such a project is that it is long-lasting, often running for years. 'It is easy to get demotivated, but what Claudia was able to do was to keep the motivation going.' The final years in particular of the Galileo project, according to Nagin Cox, 'had to be very carefully orchestrated'. This included managing the end of the project and the 'demise of the spacecraft' in order to ensure that debris was not left to litter the solar system. 'For Jupiter that meant that we needed to crash the spacecraft into the atmosphere of Jupiter, have it disintegrate as it went in.' Claudia, knowing the project as well as she did, was 'very well qualified to guide it into its final resting place'.

The audio recording of the moment captures tension, but also tears. 'OK, I cried,' said Claudia, expressing her wonder that the dying spacecraft collected data right to the end.

To run this kind of project successfully, Claudia had to coordinate large numbers of people working on multi-million-dollar projects. Nagin Cox says that her strengths lay in 'her ability to bring people together. Many of our planetary missions, in fact almost all of them, have large collaborations between international scientists, international partners, and Claudia became kind of an expert in that.' That ability, and her technical know-how, led to her being selected as European Space Agency Representative Mission US project scientist.

This was the Rosetta mission. Dr Aderin-Pocock describes how the craft travelled for over ten years in order to rendezvous with a comet. 'Getting to the comet is pretty challenging: you have got a distance of half a billion kilometres and this comet is, as we speak, coming towards the sun. So, every so often, the spacecraft has to move further away.' To obtain the data you have to get the craft as close as possible to the comet, but when the comet gets closer to the sun it outgasses, throwing off matter, 'so you need to back off every so often'. That was the challenge for the project scientist – balancing the desire for data with the possibility of the craft blowing up. It was quite a moment when the *Philae* landed on the comet. Unsurprisingly, Claudia was 'absolutely delighted', in Nagin Cox's words. 'She also, as always, found time to communicate directly with her friends and I remember getting texts with, you know, twenty exclamation points after them: "It Worked!!!!"'

Dr Aderin-Pocock describes the jubilation of the moment when she heard the news: 'It's funny, I didn't expect to feel that way, but it was just sort of, "Yes, all that work, all that effort and we've got touchdown."'

This is the kind of project that can be all-encompassing, taking over everything. But Claudia did manage to have a life outside of work. Nagin Cox says she was not the stereotypical, one-dimensional, lab-coated scientist: 'She couldn't have been further from that: she enjoyed travelling and horse-back riding. She worked very long hours and extensively on her missions, as we all do, especially at the critical milestones.'

As a woman in a male-dominated world, and a black woman in a world which is often very white, Claudia did stand out. 'Very much so,' according to Dr Aderin-Pocock. 'We have both sort of faced similar challenges in that way, but ... there is something amazing that when you join a team like that ... at first people think: "Oh yes, she is not like everybody else here, you know, she is black, and she is a woman," but I think when you get on with the science that is all people see.' Nagin Cox emphasises how 'She made time, wherever she was in the world, to give back and encourage women of colour, young women of colour, students, to pursue math and science as a fundamentally interesting field, when there are so many other things, like fame and celebrity, that draw young people, because they think that's what will be meaningful.'

In the final analysis, says Dr Aderin-Pocock, 'She was definitely a role model. I mean, she was an inspiration for me, because she just did amazing things.'

Valerie Hunter Gordon

Born 7 December 1921; died 16 October 2016, aged ninety-four

In 1947, Valerie Hunter Gordon invented the disposable nappy. Her aim was to dispense with the drudgery of washing towelling nappies for her own family, but her invention became a huge commercial success.

Valerie was the daughter of Sir Vincent de Ferranti, who founded the successful Ferranti electrical engineering company. She was married to Lieutenant-Colonel Patrick Hunter Gordon, and the couple set up home at the army training depot at Camberley in Surrey. Some episodes of *Last Word* are characterised by their humour, and in this one Valerie's son, Nigel, and daughter, Frances, spoke together to Matthew Bannister and laughed often as they talked about their mother's exploits. They started by describing her character: 'Determined, obstinate. You know; if she decided to do something then it got done,' is Frances's assessment. Both children agree that she may have inherited her inventing gene; Nigel described how her father used to come up with new inventions for household issues all the time.

'Apparently, he was determined to improve the lot of women,' says Frances, 'to take away a lot of the drudgery in life for women. And she certainly didn't like drudgery!' Valerie's own opinion of her most famous invention, the disposable nappy, was that 'it seemed extraordinary that it hadn't been done before. I thought: "Oh, that's easy, I will make them. But it wasn't easy. It was quite tricky."' The invention of the nappy was in part inspired by her son Nigel. When he was born, it was common practice for women to put their babies in rubber pants with a lining inside them, something that the medical profession disapproved of. So because she didn't want to wash nappies, Nigel says, she tried very hard to find some disposable alternative. Discovering that there simply wasn't anything 'actually made her quite angry. She got furious about it.'

The design she came up with was ingenious. Frances describes it as 'a plastic outer garment which was held at the waist with poppers and tied and adjusted around the legs with ribbon'; inside that was a disposable pad. This consisted of something akin to what loo paper is made from now, and was shaped into a wad with cotton wool on top.

It started to invite interest from other mothers she knew. Nigel explains what happened next: 'All the army wives, when she went out to army teas, asked: could you make me one of these? And it then became a full-time job, she was doing nothing but sitting around making the things.' In her own words: 'I ended up making about over 600 and I spent my time sitting at my mother's sewing machine, making these wretched things.' Valerie could see that her nappies had commercial potential. She patented her design and set about trying to interest manufacturers in the product. Eventually the Chesterfield-based company Robinson's signed a deal with her. In 1950 they sold 72,000 units, the following year a quarter of a million and, by 1963, sales had risen to 18 million packets. They decided to make them out of PVC and nylon.

When it came to the marketing, Nigel's photograph was used. He is understandably reticent on the subject, but his sister describes the 'delightful picture of him lying on his back, with his father changing his nappy, and with the garment folded very decorously over parts that needed to be covered so that they wouldn't embarrass him'. Nigel laughs as he remembers growing up used to seeing his image: 'Until I was quite old, if I was driving up and down a motorway I would see a van with a picture of myself going in the opposite direction.' Frances admits to being rather upset by this: 'A delightful photograph was also taken of me which sadly was never used because they considered his bottom was better than mine!'

The product took off, selling thousands under the brand name PADDI. The name was in fact decided on by the British Army. Frances explains that this was a result of indecision – when Valerie couldn't decide on which name to go with, she gave her husband a list just as he was going to a meeting with his Sandhurst colleagues: 'They had their meeting, all these army bigwigs, and then at the end my father said: "Could I just get you to cast your eye over these, we can't decide." So the army decided on the name "PADDI".'

Valerie went on to invent many other things, tackling anything that required lots of repetitive, boring input around the house, says Frances. She would iron by putting clothes under the carpet between sheets of newspaper, so that 'as enough people walked over them they would come out nice and flat'. She even had self-opening curtains.

She went on to redesign sanitary towels with a comfortable and secure product called the Nikini, which actually outsold the PADDI. 'As she wonderfully quoted, there were more menstruating women than there were incontinent babies in the world.' She had a huge impact on thousands of women's lives.

The last word goes to Valerie herself, who, with characteristic good humour, remarked on the way habits have a habit of changing: 'Everyone wanted to stop washing nappies, nowadays they seem to want to wash them again. Good luck to them!'

Margaret Pereira

Born 22 April 1928; died 22 December 2016, aged eighty-eight

Nowadays we are quite used to seeing a woman playing a leading role in forensic science investigations in television dramas such as Silent Witness. *But when Margaret Pereira started out as a forensic scientist in the 1950s, there was no such role model. Margaret spent much of her career at the Metropolitan Police laboratory before being appointed as the first female controller at the Home Office's Forensic Science Service.*

Her former colleague, Dr Trevor Rothwell, explained to Matthew Bannister for Last Word *that the newspapers picked up on her unusual job: 'The famous* News of the World *dubbed her "Miss Murder" because she turned up so often at the Old Bailey, giving evidence in murder cases.' She was the first woman in the biology section of that laboratory. 'She didn't encounter prejudice in her role as a laboratory worker,' he says, 'but when she decided that she wanted to report her own cases and go to court they said: "Oh no, you can't do that. Women don't do that sort of work."'*

Even when Margaret did break through this barrier, the unusual nature of being a woman in her job showed up even in the most trivial of ways. When another woman joined the Metropolitan Police laboratory, they had to share a hat. 'Because', as Dr Rothwell says, 'at that time it was rather the done thing to wear a hat when giving evidence in court.' Men, it seems, did not have to wear a hat at all.

Margaret's own description of her lab gives a good sense of the inherent strangeness of the work they undertook there: 'We have a lot of old clothing, old boots, tyres, vehicles ... You would be quite amazed if you were to look into one of our laboratories, because there we are, with the most sophisticated equipment, and all these old clothes which are the subject of very serious scientific investigation.'

Perhaps one of the most high-profile cases she was involved in concerned Lord Lucan. The murder of his children's nanny and his subsequent disappearance caused a sensation in 1974. Peter Martin worked with Margaret Pereira on the case: 'What Margaret said to me was: "Never try to get more from the results than can be substantiated in evidence in court." It's something that stuck with me the whole of my career.' In this instance 'There was a lot of blood around: in two areas, one in the basement and one in the hallway that led to the front door.' Crucially, it was necessary to do a thorough investigation to determine what the blood groups were.

Dr Trevor Rothwell takes up the story: 'She examined various items, one of which was a piece of lead pipe which was found in a car that Lucan had borrowed, and later abandoned. And that pipe had blood staining on it and the blood had come from Lord Lucan's nanny.' Her work, therefore, was 'a very substantial part of the evidence' that led to Lucan being convicted of the murder in absentia.

The work was varied. When asked what case particularly stood out in her memory, Margaret herself pointed not to a high-profile murder, but to an unusual case of child-stealing. 'On that occasion I was able to show that the child could not possibly have been the child of the woman who had it in her possession: its blood group matched perfectly with the parents who had lost the child.'

In the forensic field, she is best known for having developed a technique for determining blood groups from very, very small samples. Dr Rothwell explains the significance of this: 'Until that time, the size of bloodstain that could be examined was about the size of a penny, and she managed to invent a technique that used absolutely minute samples of blood. And this technique, which became known by her name – the Nicholls and Pereira technique – was adopted worldwide.'

According to her colleagues, Margaret never had any qualms about the more grisly aspect of her job, the fact that she was dealing with dead bodies and bloodstains, although Peter Martin does stress that 'sometimes it really did worry her as to what the ramifications of these crimes actually were.

As to whether she was a role model for other women entering the profession, Dr Rothwell is emphatic: 'Yes, there were many young women who would have regarded her as a very considerable role model.' And there is no longer any question of such women having to share a hat.

Maryam Mirzakhani

Born 12 May 1977; died 14 July 2017, aged forty

Professor Maryam Mirzakhani was the first woman to win the prestigious Fields Medal for mathematics, often seen as comparable to a Nobel Prize. She was born and brought up in post-revolutionary Iran and won two gold medals in the International Mathematical Olympiad as a teenager. She went on to take a PhD at Harvard University and then, in 2008, became a professor at Stanford University.

This episode of Last Word *takes us into the dizzyingly abstract world of mathematics; an area that can seem intimidating to all but the most mathematical of minds. In fact, her colleague Professor Jo Boaler described how Maryam herself had 'struggled with maths as a child, as everyone does, and was even told by her sixth-grade teacher that she wasn't good at maths. Fortunately for the world, she had teachers later on who believed in her.' As she points out, there is something very inspirational in the fact that someone who received such a negative message at a young age went on to become one of the most successful mathematicians in the world.*

Professor Curtis McMullen was Maryam's doctoral advisor at Harvard, and told Matthew Bannister for *Last Word* what his first impressions of Maryam were: 'She was quite humble and unpretentious. Her English was good, she was writing Farsi in her notebooks, going backwards, in these American-style notebooks.' He was struck most by her 'intense curiosity and drive'.

Professor McMullen describes her work, and how it evolved through taking an idea and developing it in dramatic ways: 'She started attending a very informal seminar on geometry and dynamics and then I asked her to report on a paper about the phenomena of counting the number of simple loops on a doughnut, on a surface with one hole. Then, to my surprise, the next week she arrived in my office and said: "I think I have an approach to doing this for surfaces with any number of holes."'

She described her own work in a way that, for non-mathematicians, sounds both exotic and fascinating: 'My main interest is understanding structures you can put on a surface; there are different ways of thinking that: either you have a surface with some additional geometric structures, or these kind of problems are related to understanding the space of such structures.' To understand a tiny fraction of what this means, it helps to envisage the work she did on the mathematics of billiards. As Professor Mc-Mullen explains, 'One of the things that might be surprising to most people is that, while we understand fairly well how a billiard ball moves about on a traditional rectangular table, already if you take a table with an L-shape it becomes quite tricky to analyse the way a billiard ball – bouncing in the usual way off of the edges – will traverse the table. Will it eventually, for example, reach every point on the table?'

It may seem that these are quite abstruse theoretical questions, but Professor McMullen explains how an understanding of complex patterns can be brought to bear on many different situations: 'They fall under the rubric of the broader field of dynamical systems, and dynamical systems is simply the theory of how things evolve in time.' This might be anything from 'the planets moving in their courses' to 'the evolution of financial markets. And this abstract theory, which seems to make little reference to real life, actually seeks to find universal laws that underlie dynamical systems.' Even, he says, 'the development of a human being from an embryo, and evolution itself' are aspects of dynamics, 'so the field she engaged in, although she engaged in the abstract end of it, is really pervasive in science'.

The work that gained her the Fields Medal was what Professor McMullen describes as 'a monumental programme'. Maryam and Alex Eskin together 'showed that the remarkable rigidity problem, which holds for ordinary matrices with ordinary numbers in them, had an echo or an analogue in this very sophisticated field of algebraic geometry and moduli spaces that record the different shapes of surfaces. So there was sort of a field where there was no linearity or matrices in evidence, and yet they found evidence of this extremely exciting rigidity phenomena in this area. So in a paper of well over 100 pages, they established this spectacular result.'

If that all sounds extremely theoretical and abstract, his description of the Fields Medal ceremony in Seoul at which she received her award paints an engagingly human picture of this enormously intelligent woman: 'She was handed the award by the president of Korea and then afterwards I gave a laudation on her work.' He was rather worried about giving this laudation, because it involved presenting her own work back to her. Luckily, though, 'she was trying to keep her very excitable daughter from disrupting the ceremony and wasn't really paying much attention to what I was saying!'

Paying tribute, Professor Jo Boaler praised Maryam's achievements and influence and pointed to the inspiration she provides to girls and women 'and all young mathematicians who believe in beautiful, visual, mathematics that can be seen and solved in different ways. Maryam is a shining light in creative mathematics and she may have been taken from us, but her light will never go out.'

Diane Leather

Born 7 January 1933; died 5 September 2018, aged eighty-five

In May 1954, Diane Leather, a twenty-one-year-old chemistry grad-uate from Streetly in Staffordshire, became the first woman to run a mile in under five minutes. The feat came only three weeks after Roger Bannister raced into the history books by breaking the four-minute-mile. But Diane Leather's name – and record – are largely unknown.

Diane had only begun running two years earlier. Inspired by the Helsinki Olympics, she joined her local athletics club and discov-ered an amazing natural talent. Sports writer Anna Kessel gives us an insight into how the record-breaking race came about: 'It was three days after she had already made an attempt and got very close.' In fact, she had run the 800 metres earlier that day; but, as Anna Kessel says, obviously 'she hadn't exhausted herself'. Unlike Roger Bannister's record attempt, Diane's took place during an actual race. 'She didn't have any pacemakers, off she set and halfway through she was leading from the front, and as she crossed the line there is this wonderful quote where she says, "Oh good, at last!"' She had made it.

In later interviews, Diane herself characteristically downplayed the moment, saying only that she knew that she must have been thrilled and excited to overcome this 'barrier that was waiting to be broken', but that she found it quite difficult to remember her precise emotions.

Roger Bannister, of course, became a household name, and yet very few people have heard of Diane Leather and her achievement. As Anna Kessel makes clear, this has nothing to do with Diane herself, but everything to do with the perception of women's sports back then. 'A lot of it has to come down to how women's running was viewed ... this wasn't a world record, because it wasn't *viewed* as a world record. Sport at the time didn't feel comfortable with women running longer distances.' As she points out, the 800 metres wasn't officially recognised until 1967, the women's marathon at the Olympics only began in 1984 and it was 2014 before they participated in the ski jump. 'So all this concern about women's wombs and what might happen if they overexert themselves was a huge factor, and so, therefore, they didn't have that official platform, and unfortunately Diane's record still isn't a record today.'

Nevertheless, her feat did attract some attention: 'There was coverage, and it is interesting that when you look back at some of the Pathé footage, she is often pictured alongside Roger Bannister. But somebody did some research into the archives and monitored the amount of newspaper coverage for Roger, and for her, over a two-year-period, 1954 to 1956, and she had something like half the amount of newspaper articles that he did.'

After Diane's record, it was another thirteen years before women were able to run the mile in international events. That came too late for her, although she set the 800-metre world record in 1955 and ran the same distance at the Rome Olympics in 1960. That year she put running behind her, to the extent that even her four children had no idea of her achievements, until her daughter Lindsey made a chance discovery: 'I found a scrapbook that one of her brothers had made, with all of her newspaper clippings and photographs in it. I was stunned, so I took it to her and asked her all about it and of course she said: "Oh, it was nothing, nothing." ... She was incredibly modest.'

She went on to have a second, very successful career as a social worker, says Lindsey, something she began in her early forties. Her career in social work was itself exceptional: 'She was working in one of the hardest parts of social work, in childcare.' After her retirement she continued to be involved by working on fostering committees for the council, and for various children's charities. 'She was extraordinary, but felt that that was just ordinary.'

Clearly Diane was a woman with an extraordinary amount of

determination, something shown even in the fact that she studied chemistry back in the 1950s. But, as her daughter puts it, this just felt natural to her. 'She was slightly intolerant of people who gnash and wail, if you like. She was a woman who just buggered on with life!'

As for how she felt about the sportswomen who came after her, she never dwelled on the recognition they got which had largely eluded her. 'She wasn't bitter, ever,' says her daughter, 'she just accepted that was the way that life was, in those days.' As perceptions of women's sport changed she felt pride and delight in their achievements, without feeling upset that she hadn't been recognised in the same way. 'It was just the way things were.' It is her daughter, in fact, who feels outraged on her behalf, 'because she really was a pioneer for women'.

Jan Morris

Born 2 October 1926; died 20 November 2020, aged ninety-four

Jan Morris was the author of more than fifty books, many chronicling her travels around the world. She also wrote novels and a bestseller called Conundrum, *which described her experience of gender reassignment in 1972.*

She was born James Morris into an Anglo–Welsh family living in Somerset, and recalled a significant childhood experience when she became a chorister at Christ Church, Oxford. This is where, she said, 'her life began', because the 'extraordinary experience' of singing every day in the cathedral, which was for her 'like a kind of showbusiness', profoundly affected her. Indeed, she later went back to Christ Church as an undergraduate.

While still living as James Morris, Jan served in the army as an intelligence officer, before starting a career in journalism and pulling one of the most dramatic scoops of the twentieth century. This was a story that made the front page of *The Times* on the morning of the Queen's coronation: Hillary and Tenzing's conquest of Everest.

Getting the scoop required some ingenuity: because of the tense political situation on the frontier, journalists weren't allowed to have radios. But realising that there was a small Indian Army radio post there, she 'devised a code in which a message appeared to be not in code. I remember the thing which said Everest had been climbed, for which the code was: "snow conditions bad".'

Jan always had ambitions to write full-length books, and the inspiration for the first one stemmed from her years in the army. Writer Paul Clements described for *Last Word* how Jan had been seconded to Venice, with a job operating boats, and escorting the generals and senior officers up and down the Grand Canal. It allowed for 'great insight into Venice ... the city and its water-ways'. Jan married Elizabeth in 1949, and went back to Venice, now with a family, to live there for six months, writing a book about the city which was published in 1960. Jan 'just loved the buildings and the history of it,' says Paul, developing 'an impressionistic sensitivity to place [which] captured the mood and the atmosphere beautifully, and the book is just full of inventiveness and linguistic originality.'

Jan preferred not to be called a travel writer, preferring to be known as someone who wrote about place. This was, Paul Clements believed, out of a desire not to be pigeonholed. 'The *Times Literary Supplement* once described her as a "motorized scholar gypsy" and I think that's a very good description of her.'

Famously, Jan also wrote about her change of gender. She and the family had been living in Oxford, says Paul Clements, and then moved to Wales, 'leading a double life effectively' by going back to Oxford during the week. Jan referred to this time as 'the androgynous years', during which time she was taking medication and changing gender, but it was not until 1972, in Casablanca, that she had the operation.

Jan herself described this part of the process as 'faintly romantic ... the surgeon was a very dashing elegant young Frenchman and there was music in the street outside, Arabic music which I love, which came through the window as I lay there waiting for this thing'. After returning from the operation as Jan, she wrote *Conundrum*. This sold in huge numbers, and it 'prompted an exceptional critical reaction from the literary establishment', says Paul Clements. It was denounced by some as being 'morally repugnant'; some feminists objected to what they saw as stereotyping women; some people were 'just completely bemused', but it also provoked acclaim and applause.

Jan's view of her own life was that she had always been a woman trapped in a man's body, ever since she was a child. She had known from the age of three or four that she had been 'born into the wrong sex and wanted to do something about it'. She went on to have four children, and in an interview on *Desert Island Discs* in 2002 she described her marriage, and how she had never kept her identity from Elizabeth: 'It wasn't just the normal sort of marriage of love and sex, it was also a marriage of friendship. We were friends from the very beginning, so I wouldn't have had any secrets from her anyway. I don't know if she had any from me, I don't think so.' Elizabeth's support was clearly integral to Jan's existence; she described her as 'the key to the latch of my conundrum' throughout their long-lasting marriage.

Another of her great books was her work about the British Empire, *Pax Britannica*. According to Paul Clements, this was 'a huge work that took fifteen years to research, and to write. It was a narrative history of storytelling of the people of the Empire and the politicians, the soldiers . . .' It was a tour de force that 'broke the limits of historical writing': 'One of the great skills of Jan Morris's writing was the sensory side.' So the book conjures up the string orchestras at dances, 'the gossip of tea parties on the lawn, the cheering crowds at race meetings, all these sorts of noises and smells came through'.

To talk to, says Paul, she was 'extremely self-deprecating. She loved to refer to herself constantly as a flibbertigibbet writer.' Right to the end of her life, she had 'a magnetic attraction about her, she still had an aura'. She had a great sense of humour, in person and on the page. Paul gives an example from a trip to Sudan, where, Jan wrote, 'the Sudanese minister of National Guidance once told me that my duty as a journalist should be to write thrilling attractive and good news, coinciding *where possible* with the truth'.

Jan's philosophy was, like everything about her, singular to her: 'I believe very much in the continuity of life, and I don't believe in death really.' She was interested in what would happen to us after death, 'and that of course is all heavily tied up with one's personal identity, with one's feeling of place, whether one belongs to a place or not, with all sorts of spiritual conceptions, which really if you look into them closely come to the great question: what is going to happen next?'

Patricia Brown

Born 1 May 1917; died 26 February 2021, aged 103

Patricia Brown was one of the leading British codebreakers during the Second World War. She worked first at Bletchley Park, and then at the German Diplomatic Section based in London's Mayfair. After the war she joined the Foreign Office, before marrying a diplomat and being posted with him to many different countries.

Patricia's daughter, Iona Brown, told *Last Word* that her mother kept her vow of silence about her wartime experiences: 'We really didn't know much about it at all until much later in life. She never spoke about it to us as children.'

Patricia was born in Dacca in what was then India but is now Bangladesh. She was the daughter of the Irish judge Sir Charles Bartley, who survived a number of assassination attempts as he carried out his work on behalf of the British Empire. Despite this, Iona says, her mother's early childhood was happy: 'It was a very romantic life out there.' Patricia's own mother seemed a very 'glamorous figure who used to go shooting tigers and was quite bewitching'. Patricia was sent back to England to go to a series of boarding schools. She was miserable at all of them and suffered dreadfully from homesickness. 'I think she told me once that she didn't see her mother for something like four years, which was extraordinary.'

Dr Tessa Dunlop, the author of a book called *The Bletchley Girls*, explained that it was a formidable woman called Emily Anderson who recruited Patricia, having noticed her fluency in languages. Patricia 'had this fluency in French and German and I think that's the key, that's why she stood out – she clearly was an exceptional woman anyway'. By a stroke of fate Anderson was lodging in

Buckinghamshire, where Patricia happened to be. Anderson, the only junior woman assistant at the Government Code and Cipher School in 1919, 'was a pretty terrifying woman, let me tell you ... and someone who really knew her onions. And she was impressed by Patricia.'

Patricia was put on to the task of cracking the code known as Floradora, named after a musical. As Dr Dunlop explains, 'the Park had so many different sections and compartmentalised areas, and there's been so much myth-making around it that we tend to think everything was Enigma encrypted or Lorenz encrypted, and all of it required a bombe machine, but actually that wasn't the case. There was a huge number of individual communications and sets of communications.' What was required was not only good brain power, but also a large measure of patience. Patricia noticed some regularities in the communications she was working on that nobody had spotted. These regularities 'vastly reduced the number of groups that needed to be decoded ... In other words she spotted patterns ... that requires patience.'

Her daughter comments that this suited the way her mother thought: 'She was very good with words, she had a very accurate observational sense, she would do the *Times* crossword in about ten minutes or something, and she did it every single day, so she was very good ... at pulling together disparate elements and making something new out of them.' The codebreaking work, though undoubtedly hard, would have been satisfying for her.

Not everything about Bletchley was congenial. According to Dr Dunlop, 'she did come up against some pretty unpleasant sexism'. Her supervisor, Frederick Freeborn, 'consistently overlooked her', something which made her feel 'very undermined'.

As a child, Patricia had been seen as arrogant by her siblings – her nickname was 'Lake Superior' because 'her nose was always in the air'. This, thinks Iona, is part of the reason why she kept the Bletchley years to herself. 'She didn't want us to feel overshadowed.' As for those regularities she spotted in Floradora, she herself said, 'I never knew the lasting significance' of the discovery, but this was partly, her daughter thinks, because she never gave much weight to her own achievements. She wasn't terribly proud of her beauty or her intelligence. She was much more interested in 'a sort of interior life that really we didn't know much about'.

From Dr Dunlop's point of view, she was someone who 'hid her light under a bushel', but this was perhaps not just because she was a modest person, but also someone who 'had a very full and accomplished life on a personal and professional level in so many ways'. She may not have been very forthcoming about Bletchley, but 'in our modern shout-it-out society, there's something incredibly dignified about that silence'.

Campaigning Women

This is a crowded field: the *Last Word* archives are brimming with the stories of women who set out to change the world in large ways and small. Whether in health, or law, or human rights, or social justice, these are women who paid attention. They had their eyes open to wrongs, and they found ways to set them right. Often they did it with humour, always with energy, sometimes at great cost to themselves.

We see it in Helen Bamber, driven to go to Belsen and then to dedicate her life to the victims of torture; we see it in Sister Ruth Pfau, who transformed the fate of people suffering from leprosy in Pakistan; in Scharlette Holdman, who spent her life fighting for those on death row. And we see it closer to home: in June Jolly bringing a lion cub into a paediatric ward to change children's experiences of hospital, or in Jill Saward, who took the most terrible experience of her young life and turned it into a campaign to help others. What these women have in common is a fearlessness in pursuing a better world. And what the *Last Word* recordings give us is the sense of what these saintly-sounding women were like as people: how it was to know them or work alongside them, or to laugh with them late into the evening while fighting the good fight.

It would be impossible to include all the campaigning women the programme has covered: they number in the hundreds. This is just a handful – the kind of women who inspire, who disrupt, who make a difference.

Nicky Chapman,
Baroness Chapman

Born 3 August 1961; died 3 September 2009, aged forty-eight

When Baroness Chapman addressed the House of Lords on disability issues the peers paid close attention. Just two feet nine inches tall and using an electric wheelchair, Nicky Chapman knew only too well what it meant to live with a disability. She was born with brittle bone disease and at her birth doctors told her parents that her life would never be worth living. But for the next forty-eight years Nicky set out to prove them wrong. She used her profile to campaign against assisted suicide legislation and fought to get better access to taxis for disabled people. After attending a school for the physically disabled, Nicky Chapman went on to a mainstream college where she studied maths and management. She committed herself to helping others, chairing a number of charities including the housing trust in Leeds that nominated her for the House of Lords. In her spare time she was a fanatical fan of Leeds United Football Club and was a familiar figure at the team's Elland Road ground.

As her brother Dan Chapman recalled for Matthew Bannister, when Nicky was born none of this could have been predicted: 'She was born with very, very, complex ... osteogenesis imperfecta, more commonly known as brittle bones, and she was born with a large number of fractures.' After doctors had examined her, they didn't think she would live through her first day. 'It looked very bleak from the outset.'

As Nicky put it herself many years later with characteristic humour: 'My parents were told that I wouldn't live more than eight hours, and then they were told that I wouldn't live more than a day, then a week, then a month, then the doctors got bored. And at seven months they sent me home to die. They're still waiting!'

Asked whether Nicky was a typically bossy big sister, Dan Chapman laughs: 'Oh good grief, yes!' As her little brother, he was on the receiving end of her sharp tongue.

But Nicky was certainly fragile. According to her brother, by the time she was in her forties had had about 600 fractures. 'It was seldom that she didn't have her arm in a sling, or one of her bones had been broken by something or other.' Even the simple act of turning over in bed could cause a fracture if she wasn't careful.

Nicky herself recalled that, of her parents, it was her mother who was the more protective. Her father was more likely to encourage her to get on with things. 'I think they obviously worried, but they knew that if I was going to cope, I had to do whatever I could, you know, get out there and get amongst people.' Which is what she did.

It was at Elland Road that she was probably happiest – a place where she could relax and experience pure enjoyment, 'and really be the Nicky Chapman that everybody knew', as her brother puts it. Or as she herself said: 'I can't tell you the number of hours that I have sat on cold, wet touchlines watching football.' It was, she said, 'in the family blood'.

She was appointed to the House of Lords in 2004, nominated by the Habinteg Housing Association, of which she was chair, as a 'People's Peer'. She was, says her brother, 'absolutely stunned, and I think she was possibly the only one who was'. The family was both proud and pleased with the nomination, but perhaps not really surprised when she was appointed. 'I just had this sneaking feeling that, with Nicky, she'd achieve it, because she tended to do what nobody expected you would ever believe could be done.'

Baroness Chapman's fellow disability campaigner, Baroness Finlay, also spoke to Matthew Bannister, and described the reaction Nicky got within the House of Lords: 'She came into the Lords, and I think everybody initially was really quite shocked to see the extent of her disability.' But their main impression was her ability to cope and the smile on her face. 'She inspired people with a zest for life and this smile . . . and her ability to joke against herself, joke against her situation, and find humour and laughter in the most serious situations.'

Baroness Finlay was particularly struck by a speech she made in 2006, when she said: 'People who are injured, or develop a condition, often speak of how they assumed they would not, or could not, enjoy life any more. This is when they are at their most vulnerable, and death can seem the only solution for all concerned. And then she went on to say how it can take a long time for people to adapt, and how, from her own experience, the human spirit can win through, and people begin to value life and enjoy the rest of their life again. And that was very powerful, because, of course, she had been there herself.'

Asked whether Nicky was a person in a hurry, conscious that time was against her, Baroness Finlay describes her as 'a woman who knew that we all live with uncertainty every day of our lives, and that we need to value every moment of our lives, because we just don't know what's coming next. So she had confronted the uncertainty that most of us try to avoid.' While we like to believe we have some control in our lives, she lived with the knowledge that there were things which she simply could not change.

Patricia Stephens Due

*Born 9 December 1939; died 7 February 2012, aged
seventy-two*

*Patricia Stephens Due was a leading American civil rights activist.
She first came to national prominence during a student protest in the
1960s in her native state of Florida, and she spent the rest of her life
campaigning for the rights of the oppressed.*

*Her daughter, Tananarive Due, talked to Matthew Bannister about
her mother, and laughed as she said that even as a schoolgirl Patricia
was stirring things up: 'Mom always told the story about feeling that
her high school principal was not functioning up to his level of responsibility. So she actually started a petition to try to oust him.' Her aim was
to attempt to ensure that her fellow black pupils would be ready for the
moment when schools were integrated, but 'the kids were so petrified
that they would get in trouble that they actually chased her in school to
try to get their names off of the petition'.*

Dr Paul Ortiz is the director of the Samuel Proctor Oral History
Program at the University of Florida. He describes Florida as one of
the toughest of the segregationist states, a place with a higher rate
of lynchings than Mississippi: 'Most of the political leadership were
supporters of white supremacy; it was known by many African-
Americans as "America's Siberia". So, when Patricia Stephens Due
began her activism and work in the civil rights movement, it took a
real courageous group of people to really to begin to do that.'

Early on in her activist career, Patricia was injured during a
demonstration while leading a march of students in support of
the Congress of Racial Equality – CORE – of which she was a
founding member. She was tear-gassed by the police. According

to Tananarive: 'She had a tear gas canister lobbed into her face and [afterwards] experienced great sensitivity to light, even indoor light, so she wore dark glasses.' But even with this injury she showed no signs of being cowed. Her attitude was '"OK, so I will wear these glasses, and I will keep marching on, I am still going to lie down in front of this garbage truck during a sanitation workers' strike." And whatever needed doing, she just seemed to deal with.'

She spelled out in an interview what it was like to be in the forefront of the civil rights movement: 'We had been foot soldiers, actually in a war heaped on us by our own country. And I had one of the wounds that was visible, but there were many wounds that you could not see. There were so many emotional wounds.' She said that as she was led away, blinded, to a church to recover, she could still hear the screams of the other students. 'So what you did was important, and you had to do it because you had to make a difference, and in my case, I had to be free.'

Her next step, says Tananarive, was to organise sit-ins at white-only establishments in Tallahassee. This was part of the sit-in movement that spread across the South in early 1960. What the sit-ins were asking for seems like such a basic human right: for black people to be treated like any other citizens in restaurants. But the words of a white member of the public, recorded at the time, give a harsh and sobering sense of what the civil rights activists were up against: 'They come in, and we are not used to them sitting down beside us because I wasn't raised with them. I never have lived with them. And I am not going to start now.'

Opposition to the sit-ins grew, and violence flared. Dr Ortiz described what Patricia did next: 'Up to that point civil activists arrested or held by the police would generally get bailed out. Patricia Stephens Due, and her sister Priscilla, and several of the other activists decided to refuse to pay the fine.' She went on to serve forty-nine days. Her reasoning was that 'by sacrificing her freedom, she would shine a light on the conditions of oppression that were being experienced by black people in Florida'.

Tananarive described how this action by Patricia resonated: 'It became the first jail-in. The baseball great Jackie Robinson, who at that time had a column in the *New York Post*, published a letter that my mother wrote from the jail, so it gave them a national platform. He sent all of the participants diaries, so that they could keep track of their time there.' Dr Martin Luther King Junior himself sent them a telegram.

As Dr Ortiz describes it: 'People like Eleanor Roosevelt, James Baldwin, Harry Belafonte noticed what this young woman had courageously done.' But as recognition for her actions grew, there was a backlash: 'The state was infuriated . . . the FBI began shadowing her, but also the Board of Control pushed her college to actually prevent her from continuing on with her education.'

Patricia continued as an activist for the rest of her life, organising community and labour workshops and being active in unions. As a mother, says Tananarive, she put all the fierceness of her activism into her children. She was a 'Mommy Tiger'. The energy she had invested in public protest was transferred into the domestic sphere and into her children: 'In some cases the teachers were too intimidated to call her when we were in trouble, because they felt that they would be in trouble.'

She lived to see an African-American in the White House. It's hard to overstate the significance to her of that event. As Tananarive puts it: 'It was absolutely amazing, because activists tend to look at all that remains to be done, and if you get a group of them together, they are grousing about disparities of education and disparities in economics. And all of that is true, but when your nation is electing a black president you really, as an activist, have to stand up and say: *that* is something that I never expected to see in my lifetime.'

Mabel Cooper

Born 10 August 1944; died 22 March 2013, aged sixty-eight

Mabel Cooper drew on her own terrible experiences to campaign for changes to the way people with learning disabilities are treated. Diagnosed at the age of thirteen, she spent the first part of her life in institutions. Once she emerged into the community at the age of thirty-three, she became chair of a group called London People First, giving evidence to ministers and appearing at conferences and in the media.

Her own words, dignified and clear, give a sense of why she wanted to make sure her story was told: 'I think this story is to tell people that it is wrong to shut people with learning difficulties away.'

Mabel's friend and advocate, Jane Abraham, spoke to Matthew Bannister for *Last Word* and emphasised how important Mabel found it to get this message across: 'She was very keen to tell her story, which was about a child who went into care at a few weeks old, and basically spent her childhood in children's homes and then went to one of the big institutions, St Lawrence's [Hospital] in Caterham.' She was eleven when she went to this 2,000-strong institution, and remained for twenty years. In her own words: 'They called us hurtful names like idiots, and moral defectives.' She spoke of the noise, the screaming: 'When you're eleven and you go into these big buildings, into something like St Lawrence's, it's very frightening, you would think you were going to a madhouse, because of the noise.'

Dorothy Atkinson met Mabel while studying the history of disability for the Open University. Realising that Mabel didn't know much about her early life, Dorothy helped her to research the records which revealed more of her story. What she discovered was heart-rending: she had been taken in by the authorities when she was only four weeks old, because her mother was begging on the streets of Islington. 'Her mother was sent to the hospital in Kent and she ran away from there after a few weeks and was never seen or heard of again. And Mabel went into a series of children's homes, only one of which she could remember, but we discovered she had been in six or seven different places during the whole of her childhood.'

Learning disability is a broad term that can encompass a range of conditions. Dorothy Atkinson explained that in Mabel's case it was that she seemed unable to learn to read and write as a child. But Dorothy is clear that if circumstances had been different, Mabel could have learned: 'Yes, indeed, I think she would have learned to read and write, because in later life she began to do so.'

When she came out of St Lawrence's after twenty years, in 1977, Mabel hardly spoke at all, because, said Dorothy, 'if you spoke you got shouted at, so she only used two words: yes and no, and mostly no. But when she came out, again she was quiet and silent for a while, and then started going to Croydon People First and began, just in a small way, to participate and then, as her confidence grew, she ended up becoming the leader.'

It's not surprising that adjusting to life outside the hospital was difficult. Mabel herself described it as 'very frightening. Very frightening when you come out of a hospital, after being there for twenty years. We had to learn to get on a bus, or learn to get on a train,' and this was compounded by the fact that she couldn't read. It took her, she said, a long time to learn to do these things.

In 1997 Mabel's story was one of those included in a book that Dorothy Atkinson co-authored, *Forgotten Lives*. This got a big response from the public, says Dorothy, and it led to invitations for Mabel to go to conferences, or to speak to different groups. Jane Abraham says that Mabel was particularly keen to work with children: 'One of the things that she found was that children could be bullied. We managed to get some funding to do a project going into schools, for her to tell her story, to actually encourage children to see that people may be slower, they may have disabilities, but they are people first.' Her mission was to bring understanding of what life was like inside institutions. She came into the BBC to go on *Breakfast*: 'People outside, they don't understand [about institutions]; unless you get people like me what's been in them, then nothing will change, because the people outside, they don't know.'

In 2010 the Open University gave her an honorary degree. Not surprisingly, this was a huge moment for her. Dorothy Atkinson describes it as 'a very special day in her life, because we were on stage and it was a huge audience of graduates, and academics, and families'. Mabel listened to a speech about herself and then gave an acceptance speech herself – a milestone in her life..

As to Mabel's legacy, Jane Abraham says: 'I think she made an absolutely *huge* impact. I have had several emails from people who say: "Mabel's influence on us was just profound, in terms of our own thinking about people's learning disabilities and what they can do, and also how people had been treated in the past, and how people need to be treated as equals now."'

She would be justified in being angry about what had happened to her. And, says Jane Abraham: 'In some ways she was. But she always used her anger very constructively. When St Lawrence's closed, she was invited as a guest of honour ... to press the button to blow it up. And she was very keen to make sure that institutions like that completely disappeared, that no way, at any time, could we actually go back to that.'

Helen Bamber

Born 1 May 1925; died 21 August 2014, aged eighty-nine

Helen Bamber devoted her life to working with victims of torture. She was an early member of Amnesty International and strove passionately to support prisoners of conscience. In 1985 she started the Medical Foundation for the Care of Victims of Torture. Since then it has helped more than 50,000 people from over ninety countries. At the age of eighty she set up another foundation, the Helen Bamber Foundation, to aid victims of human trafficking, domestic violence and other human rights abuses.

Helen was born in London into a Jewish family, and as the executive director of the Helen Bamber Foundation, T. J. Birdi, explained to *Last Word*, her childhood was overshadowed by politics: 'She essentially grew up in an environment where she saw the rise of fascism. She watched Mosley's blackshirts marching through London and it terrified her as a child.' Her father was keen to impress upon her the dangers of Adolf Hitler: 'He was obsessed, in her words, about what was happening, and he would read to her from *Mein Kampf* and he would translate the Nazi speeches that were being heard on the radio.' This had a huge effect on Helen as a young girl. 'Her father and her mother had a very unhappy marriage. She was an only child. But it was almost the despair of her father that she found so overwhelming. And it was partly in response to that that she felt that she had to do something.' That something was to take action: to go to Germany herself. In her own words: 'I felt as the war began to draw to an end that I would have to go to Germany and work in the former concentration camps. And I do not know how, or why. It felt inevitable and I was afraid. I wasn't sort of filled with mission and courage, I mean I was absolutely terrified.'

According to T. J. Birdi, Helen used to say that it was in the camps that she learned the most important lessons of her life, and would tell a story of how one day she saw something that she thought was just a piece of cloth blowing in the wind. She realised as she drew nearer that it was actually 'a woman, who was rocking back and forth, and who was very close to death'. Helen sat down next to her, and the woman 'grabbed hold of her and rocked back and forth with her and rasped her story'. Helen, without knowing what to do, spoke to the woman and said, 'I cannot change what has happened, and I cannot bring back those you have lost, but what I can do is bear witness to your story and your story will be told.'

Helen's own words describing the horror of the camps bring them to terrible life:

> My most vivid memory of Belsen, and Germany, was of people who would grab hold of you and take your hand, and dig their nails deep into your hand, and tell you their story, sobbing – but not sobbing with tears, but sort of from their guts, from their throats. Just telling you their story, the horror of what had happened, their losses, what had happened to them, over and over again.

When she returned from Germany she was appointed chair of the Committee of Children from the Concentration Camps. This made her responsible for looking after 722 children. These were very badly damaged children, says T. J. Birdi, 'who had seen the destruction of their families. They had been required to clear the gas chambers, they were forced labour.' She describes how, with every person she interacted with, Helen would 'explore every horror, every nightmare, and find eventually in the end – and sometimes this might take years ... "the way to survive through creative survival. To find the remnants of resilience and courage".' It was highly upsetting work; however, as Helen said, 'I would be worried if we were no longer distressed, but it's also very rewarding to see people's dignity ... people's sense of identity returning.'

She was, says T. J. Birdi, 'Brilliant. Relentless.' Her work ethic was huge, all the time until she retired. 'She was fearless if she had to be, because she was ambitious in the pursuit of compassion.' By being all these things, she 'managed to change so much for tens of thousands of people'. She was someone who improved lives. Her work sprang from the injustices she had witnessed, and what she achieved was 'phenomenal, remarkable ... She is a heroine in so many people's lives.'

Outside of work, she had her joys – 'music, jazz, was one of her greatest loves. And dancing, listening, drinking gin, laughing, chatting, intellectual discourse, poetry, art ... She loved all of the things that she said affirmed life and love.'

Perhaps her philosophy is best summed up by the contribution she made to a book called *99 Words*, which sought wisdom from various public figures. It asked a simple question: if you have breath for no more than ninety-nine words, what would those words be? Helen Bamber's ninety-nine words give an insight into everything that she built her life on. Reflecting on why she had given her life's work to helping people to deal with the effects of war and trauma, she gave the simple answer, 'Why not?', but expanded it into a brief but moving elegy about suffering, about the limits of compassion, about society, about strangers and about humanity. In the end, the real answer was love.

Efua Dorkenoo

Born 6 September 1949; died 18 October 2014, aged sixty-five

Efua Dorkenoo was a tireless campaigner against the practice of female genital mutilation – FGM – which is traditional in some African communities and affects millions of women around the world. She was born in Ghana but moved to the UK at the age of seventeen, and first encountered FGM while working as a staff nurse in London. It was partly as a result of her campaigning that it was made illegal in the UK in 1985.

For six years, in the late 1990s, Efua worked at the World Health Organisation, coordinating regional action plans against FGM in six African countries. For *Last Word* Matthew Bannister spoke to Jacqui Hunt, head of the London branch of the women's rights organisation Equality Now, who got to know her because of her campaigning, and to whom she is 'legendary . . . her work on FGM has just blazed a trail for so many years'.

In Efua's early years of campaigning, FGM was a hidden issue. Jacqui Hunt starts by describing the practice: 'Various parts of a girl's genitalia are cut, and that can cause death through bleeding and infection; it can cause difficulty in childbirth and there are lots of psychological and other harmful effects, fistula as well. It is really about controlling the chastity of the girls, it is like a medieval chastity belt, that is the idea behind it.'

Efua came across this practice in the UK 'because she was a nurse, and she did some midwifery training, and she noticed that women who had FGM were finding birth very, very, difficult'. Efua's own measured description of how that discovery affected her gives a visceral sense of how traumatic FGM is: 'I had to deal with a woman who had the most extensive FGM and was totally closed. The cries of that woman giving birth and this life-saving channel for humans blocked, and her screaming, and professionals around not knowing anything about it, really touched me.'

Having made this discovery, Efua's mission was to change things. According to Jacqui Hunt: 'She was like a force of gravity, she pulled people towards her.' This included young girls from those communities that practise FGM: 'They were completely inspired by her.'

Matthew also spoke to one of the many young girls she had helped, Nimco Ali, an FGM survivor who was encouraged by Efua to speak publicly about what happened to her. Nimco, who as CEO of the Five Foundation, the global partnership to end FGM, is now a leading activist in this area, says that Efua helped her cope with the resulting abuse and the isolation: 'She was the first person that looked like my grandmother who would talk about African women's sexuality.'

When Nimco began to talk about her own experience and to campaign, she and Efua went out to dinner to celebrate a piece in the *Evening Standard*. 'Efua said: "This is what it is about, not only will this set you free, but it will also help thousands of girls out there." And I remember the first horrible text message came, and because she was sitting in front of me, I could actually reply back and say to this person, who was very close to me – like a relative: "Why don't you have your genitals fully removed and get back to me?" Efua brought a sense of security that 'allowed me to bring that fierceness out. She was very fierce, she really didn't care whether it was snowing, whether it was raining, she would just be banging on doors; and whenever somebody said something, she would just turn the other cheek.' During a difficult period in Nimco's life, when her own family had withdrawn from her due to her campaigning, 'She was that surrogate mother, but my mother came back, and my grandmother came back.' One of their last conversations, in fact, was about Nimco's family, and about 'the fact that my mother was now anti-FGM, and she said: "If we have achieved anything, that's a great thing."'

Efua was a leading expert on FGM, writing about the practice. She was working on a second book when she died. In her first book, according to Jacqui Hunt, 'she was one of the first people who termed FGM a human rights abuse. A lot of people thought it was a cultural issue and, therefore, it was OK for it to be practised by some cultures, and she just said: "No, how would you react if it was your daughter?" She insisted on having it incorporated in the child protection system.'

By the time of her death, says Jacqui Hunt, it finally felt like all the work that she had put in over the years was beginning to bear fruit. She would sometimes become frustrated that the struggle – which she had been involved in for thirty years – was taking so long. 'But I think, just in the last year or two ... her efforts, and those of others also, were paying off enormously. Her legacy will live on in many countries.'

It seems fitting to give the last word on Efua to one of the many girls she helped so much, Nimco Ali: 'She was the stone that kind of created the ripple effect, which means that millions of girls across the world won't be cut. I don't think she has gone, because she has left so much behind. That's going to be the thing that I am going to console myself with, that she is still carrying on her work, but somewhere else.'

Debbie Purdy

Born 4 May 1963; died 23 December 2014, aged fifty-one

Debbie Purdy was diagnosed with primary progressive multiple sclerosis in 1995 and campaigned on two fronts thereafter: to ensure the right to die; and, if that wasn't possible, to clarify what others could legally do when a patient is close to death. On the latter she won a landmark legal ruling in 2009, which led to the issuing of new guidelines on assisted suicide. Backers praised her as a valued campaigner, but critics raised fears that the elderly and vulnerable could be put under pressure to agree to end their lives.

Debbie Purdy's campaign began out of concern for her husband, Omar Puente, who she believed might eventually have to help her end her life. In the same year as her court victory she and her husband appeared on *Woman's Hour*, where she described how they met when she was sent to go and cover his band in Singapore: 'He was told to be nice to me, and he was.' Omar's account complemented hers – to an extent: 'I had been told that a journalist was going to interview me, and she came there, and you know really nice, and you know fresh, and she was all over me.' 'So he says!' retorted Debbie, laughing.

Emma Glasbey is a BBC *Look North* reporter who followed Debbie Purdy's story closely. Julian Worricker spoke to her for *Last Word*, starting by asking about the relationship between Debbie and Omar. 'It was a very strong relationship,' says Emma, 'a relationship that started under such unusual circumstances. When they met Debbie was a music journalist, sent to interview Omar. She spoke no Spanish, Omar spoke very little English, but they fell in love.' However, Debbie was at the start of a very different story – at the same time, the first symptoms of multiple sclerosis were starting to manifest. 'She was diagnosed with primary progressive multiple sclerosis within weeks of their relationship starting.' But they didn't let this get in their way. 'Debbie told me once that she was having problems with her legs and she used to step on to Omar's feet, so they could dance around.' The couple travelled the world, but as Debbie's condition got worse they returned to Bradford. 'They had a very active, a very busy life.' Omar worked as a jazz musician, and they both became involved in her campaigning mission to clarify the law.

As for Debbie's own personality: 'Well, she was *very* intelligent, she had a keen interest in politics, in news, she loved to debate with people . . . I think even her opponents liked her because she was so interesting to talk to. She had a fabulous sense of humour even in the most difficult times, even over the past year as she was in the hospice you could share a joke with her . . . And of course there were a lot of opponents, because there was a lot of concern about her campaign.' What Debbie wanted first of all was clarity about the law, but her ultimate goal was to change it. This was something that some people – the old, people with disabilities – found very alarming. 'They felt it would make them vulnerable, they might feel a burden, they might feel obliged to use this law.'

Such a controversial campaign inevitably aroused some quite personal issues. Debbie dealt with this by being as open as possible to the opposing point of view, says Emma: her modus operandi was to talk not only to her supporters, but also to those on the other side of the fence: 'She wanted to talk to people about how important safeguards were if the law were ever to be changed.' As she went through her own struggle, with doctors trying out different drugs and physiotherapy and psychiatrists, 'she always felt that anyone who wanted to end their life would have to be made to go through a process like that'.

In the *Women's Hour* interview, Debbie outlined her mission: her point was that if assisted dying could become legal, and supported by physicians, then 'If somebody needs counselling, if somebody needs a change in pain medication, if somebody needs a difference in their social situation, that can be explored.'

And she also spoke about the internal struggle: what it is like to be forced to think about the day that you die. 'It is really difficult, and the fact that we don't talk about it all the time doesn't mean that I don't think about it a lot, but the two things in life that are absolutely guaranteed are taxes and death. Everybody will face this at some point, everybody has to face death, but I don't want to be defined by my multiple sclerosis and I don't want to be defined by the fact that my life could become intolerable. Everybody has to face these things, but you just have to know that it has to happen.'

Assisted suicide remains illegal, but by the time she died, after a year in a hospice, Debbie had transformed the debate about the end of life.

Jeanne Córdova

Born 18 July 1948; died 10 January 2016, aged sixty-seven

Jeanne Córdova was a former nun who became a prominent writer and campaigner for lesbian rights. Based in California, she started Lesbian Tide *magazine, which eventually had a national and international readership.*

Jeanne was the second of twelve children in a devout Catholic family. For *Last Word* Matthew Bannister spoke to her sister Lu, who described how their crowded childhood taught Jeanne her leadership skills: 'Well, Jeanne was able to command ten people under her – to do everything from who's going to eat their vegetables to what TV shows we were going to watch.' It was a traditional household where the young were expected to respect their elders. It was also very religious, and Jeanne grew up to feel she was 'very much in love, with God, and Mary, and all that, and I probably was'. Subconsciously, though, she would later say that she was also trying to avoid marriage, and the convent seemed like the only alternative.

Her spouse, Lynn Harris Ballen, thinks it is significant that she chose to join a relatively social-justice-based order of nuns: 'They opposed the Vietnam War, they had Bob Dylan come to sing for the novices, they had priests on the run from the FBI who were opposing the war come and hide at the mother house.' It was ideal training for being an activist. Still, it wasn't long before she worked out that perhaps the convent was not the correct calling for her. According to her sister, 'I believe it was twenty-four hours! I think that she no sooner stepped foot in the nunnery than she realised that she had indeed been called to something, but perhaps it was not God.'

What she did find in the convent, according to Lynn, 'was a community of women'. At some level, she was aware that such a community was the right place for her. In spite of her traditional upbringing, she never felt that her sexuality was problematic: 'She actually thought that what she felt was so right, obviously the Church must be wrong.'

Emerging from the convent, Jeanne looked around for like-minded people, eventually coming across a lesbian organisation called the Daughters of Bilitis or 'DOB'. She herself described how she went about her search, remembering that a good place to find 'gay-looking women' was on softball teams. But she got bored with that, and wanted to find lesbians who were interested in literature or politics. Walking down the steps of a church to the basement where the DOB was meeting, Jeanne said: 'I remember seeing organised women sitting around talking about homosexuality and they're talking about the government, and they're talking about someday not living this way, in a basement. And I was thrilled.'

She went on to found *Lesbian Tide* from within the DOB, says Lynn Harris Ballen, though she moved it on from there when it became too radical for them. 'It was both a very professional news magazine and it was also very much a community magazine, and a place where lesbian culture – the early music, the first books, all of that – were being talked about.' She also published a community yellow pages – a directory helping to bring gay and lesbian business-es to wider attention, because she felt that the community needed services that understood them and their needs. She ensured that all the advertisers were at least gay-friendly, if not LGBT them-selves. There was an ulterior motive to this: she saw 'that so many of these gay professionals were closeted, and she felt that if she gave them a place to come out in a more business-oriented context, then when they came out they would all be willing to donate to the causes'.

Lu Córdova identifies what drove Jeanne: 'I think Jeanne thought of her life as one that served people, and I think that was what she was the most proud of.' Lynn Harris Ballen echoes this, describing her as someone who lived her life through her principles: 'She wasn't somebody who just talked about doing things; she always put her words into action.'

June Jolly

Born 28 September 1928; died 12 March 2016, aged eighty-seven

Unusually, Matthew Bannister opened this episode of Last Word *with a very personal recollection of his own, one that conjures a huge shift in our attitudes to children: 'In 1959, when I was two and a half years old, I had a traumatic experience. I had to go into hospital for a minor hernia operation. On the steps of the building a nurse snatched me away from my mother and told her that she could go no further. I was distraught, and only stopped crying when the anaesthetic took hold.'*

It was experiences like these that Nurse June Jolly wanted to change. She pioneered a transformation on children's wards and wrote a handbook to inspire others to follow. Working at St Thomas's, and then Brook Hospital in London, June drew on her experience as a child social worker. Matthew spoke to Sue Burr, a former nurse advisor for children at the Royal College of Nursing, who worked alongside June. She reinforced how dissimilar the treatment of children was in those days: 'When June started training, life was very different for children in hospital. Many children's wards restricted visiting, even for parents, to maybe an hour a day. And children were kept in bed and they stayed in hospital much longer.' In many hospitals, visitors were only allowed twice a week. 'June was a champion of not only having free visiting for parents – and mothers of younger children staying there – but they became part of the ward team, instead of being shut out.'

June's niece, Margaretta Jolly, describes how horrified June was when she first entered the profession. Her experience as a social worker before becoming a nurse allowed her to see the standard practice through different eyes, as 'really a new form of deprivation from her point of view. She used to say, "Yes, children are cared for physically better than they ever have been, but emotionally, spiritually, it was an absolute desert." And that was the whole impetus behind her wish to bring in play, and fun, and games, and I suppose a kind of child psychology to her work.'

June's own words give a sense of how forward-thinking her schemes were at the time: 'You see, I approached it from such a different point of view.' She felt sympathetic towards the nurses, because the policy wasn't their fault – they didn't know. 'They said goodbye to the mother at the door, they took the child's clothes off, put her in something that didn't belong to her – she looked awful – sat her in a cot. And that was it. They didn't really even play until they were better.'

What June came up with, says Sue Burr, was a 'ward granny scheme', whereby there would be someone there to visit the children whose parents weren't able to come often.

Following on from this, she undertook other initiatives – bringing in rocking horses, and 'Wendy houses which could be made into little hospital houses. She said they were a must for any children's ward … she had a theory about how this would allow children to re-find the privacy that they needed to act out fears.'

One of the more eye-catching ideas she had was to bring a baby elephant on to the ward, says Margaretta: 'She had been thinking what to do at Christmas for these children. So, I think she contacted London Zoo, who said, unsurprisingly: "Well, we don't lend out our animals." But she then got in touch with an animal trainer who said: "Yes, I can provide a baby elephant and a baby lion." So all I know is that this elephant was taken on to the ward … and the lion!'

Throughout all of these schemes, she met with resistance; the feeling was that play did not matter, and that her ideas were too disruptive or expensive to be considered. June's own description of the resistance she constantly came up against illustrates this: 'Even after I had been in charge I still had to fight theatres, anaesthetists, surgeons, matrons. They didn't believe that this mattered. They were doing a good job, the children got better, everything was very clean and tidy. What does that mean to a child whose mummy's gone and left him?'

Of course, child nursing has now changed irrevocably – what June was fighting for has become the norm; the old model seems almost unthinkable, in part because of June herself. For her niece, June was 'a real role model as a woman who was not married, in fact had chosen not to have children herself'. She used to say that she wasn't married because she didn't want to have a henpecked husband. While she wouldn't have called herself a feminist, 'she was just a very strong woman who was always a rock for us and for me'.

Sue Burr sums up her character, and the effects that her determination had: 'When June set about doing something she was determined to change things and today, when you see the atmosphere in the wards now, June was at the beginning of that change and was a champion of it.' And what a champion she was.

Ruth Gruber

Born 30 September 1911; died 17 November 2016, aged 105

Ruth Gruber was a photojournalist and author. Hers is a story of seven decades spent as a correspondent in Europe and the Middle East. She once said of her typewriter and camera: 'I have two tools to fight injustice: words and images.' Born in Brooklyn in 1911 to Jewish immigrants, she was a brilliant student, completing her PhD at just twenty, before going on to cover some of the most historic events of the Second World War era. Her 1944 journey from Italy to New York on board a ship carrying refugees from concentration camps was turned into a television series.

Ruth's daughter Celia spoke to Kate Silverton for *Last Word*, and vividly conjures her mother's charisma and sense of justice: 'She was striking, and she was very elegant: it was very important for her to be dressed up. When she was representing other people she was fearless, and marvellous, and short, and great!'

Ruth saw herself as a witness in an era of barbarities and war. She documented Stalin's gulags, life in Nazi Germany, and the plight of Jewish refugees. She worked for the Department of the Interior during the Roosevelt administration and learned that Roosevelt was planning to bring over 1,000 refugees; the transport ship the *Henry Gibbins* left Naples carrying 982 Jewish refugees bound for America in July 1944. Hearing this, Ruth was emphatic: 'Somebody has to go and hold their hand: these people are going to be terrified.'

According to her daughter, the refugees came from many different countries, but Ruth was able to talk to most of them: 'Some had been in concentration camps and escaped, and they spoke different languages, but my mother spoke German and Yiddish and could communicate with them.' It was a potentially perilous journey for a great many reasons, not least that the waters were patrolled by German submarines. Ruth herself described how 'at one point, three Nazi planes ... flew over us. Word came immediately: everyone to their bunks!'

But, having seen the refugees arrive in the USA, Ruth Gruber did not leave the story there, said Celia Gruber: 'They were supposed to go back to Europe at the end of the war, and my mother worked very hard, with Eleanor Roosevelt, to get then President Harry Truman to give the right to stay.' It turned out to be a complicated situation: he couldn't simply counteract the original command, so they went first to Canada, and then from there immigrated into the USA.

Another defining moment in Ruth Gruber's life came in 1947. Working in Haifa, she heard about the now infamous passage of the *Exodus* steamship, carrying 5,000 former concentration camp survivors who were hoping to enter Palestine illegally. The British refused them permission to disembark, the ship was boarded at sea by the British Navy, and a battle broke out on her decks, resulting in casualties on both sides. The navy sent the ship first to Cyprus, where Ruth Gruber went to meet it, and then on to Port-de-Bouc in France to be deported back to Germany, where she boarded it. Her daughter described what she did: 'She got on to the ship and she started taking pictures, and it was very dark, and she couldn't even see what she was doing. But she understood that she needed to take these pictures and she needed to show them to the world.' Having taken the pictures, she approached the *Herald Tribune*, which published them. Her most famous image shows a deck full of people, caged in by barbed wire, under a Royal Navy flag on which they have superimposed a swastika. It is a powerful and shocking image: 'These strong young men were defiant, they raised that flag, they had painted the swastika on the Union Jack. They would defy, not the British Empire, they would defy the whole world.'

Following Ruth's pictures in the *Herald Tribune*, there was an international outcry that shamed the British. For Ruth, it was important that she wasn't just an observer to history, but that she was living the story too, and that she had highlighted the plight of so many people, particularly those on that steamer. Her daughter says she was proud of the effect she had had, and had 'felt *compelled* to do this'.

Ruth explained this compulsion simply: 'I think the truth can make us free. I keep searching for the truth.'

Jill Saward

Born 14 January 1965; died 5 January 2017, aged fifty-one

> *'I want people to be able to understand just how much of a trauma rape is. And I hope that what I have done will help other people.'*
>
> Jill Saward

In 1986, a shocking case of sexual violence made headline news nation-wide. Three men broke into a vicarage in Ealing, beating up the vicar and his daughter's boyfriend, and raping the vicar's daughter at knife-point. Public indignation at the event was vocal and widespread. And at the centre of it all was Jill Saward, the vicar's daughter, then twenty-one years old. The attack changed her life forever. She had nightmares and flashbacks for three years, she split up with her boyfriend and had a short-lived first marriage. But she also became a public campaigner for the rights of those who suffer sexual violence and offered help and support to many of them.

In 1990 Jill Saward published a book about her experiences called *Rape: My Story*. For *Last Word*, Matthew Bannister spoke to Jill's second husband, the journalist Gavin Drake. He described their first meeting, at the Christian arts festival, Greenbelt: 'I walked into the hospitality tent and she was sat on the same table as my editor and I didn't know who she was, but I took one look at her and thought: "I don't know who you are, but I am going to marry you." People talk about love at first sight, and in this case it really was.'

By this time Jill was already a public figure, used to talking about her ordeal. She had written her book and taken part in a celebrated BBC *Everyman* programme. As Gavin says, 'What everybody refers to as her "waiving her right to anonymity" – of course that had effectively been taken away from her already by the press.' So by the time they met she was quite comfortable discussing the rape; it was Gavin who found it disconcerting. But, as he puts it, 'Jill made it very easy. I bought her book because I thought: I need to know more about you. And it was quite difficult because Jill is a funny person, she is a very amusing person, and a lot of humour comes through in her book. So there I am sat at New Street Railway Station in Birmingham reading a book called *Rape: My Story* and laughing, and people are giving me very weird looks, because it is not appropriate to laugh when you are reading a book about such a difficult subject.'

She became a very public campaigner for changes in the law and was successful, but there was a lot of private activity too. She would reach out to help others who had survived such an ordeal. Gavin describes this part of her work as 'in some ways quite unprofessional – she never called herself a counsellor, she was quite clear that she wasn't a counsellor. She was an advisor, a supporter, an advocate. But what she wanted to do was to bring joy to people.' Her help ranged from providing practical and caring support in their darkest moments to being a source of fun and joy.

For Jill, helping people to deal with their trauma by bringing it into the open was the most important thing. 'You have to bury it and bury it dead, but the only way that you can do that is to talk about it, to talk it all through, to get it out of your system, to talk until it doesn't hurt any more and that way you can bury it dead.' She herself had 'buried it dead'.

One realisation that emerged in the week or so after Jill's death was the sheer number of people that she was communicating with, victims of rape and others. Gavin describes thousands of messages from people across the world. Even he had no idea quite how many people she was supporting: 'A picture is painted of Jill as this sort of, almost the saintliest of saints. And she was very special. But she was also somebody who did it at great cost in terms of the effect some of it had on her ... driving her through that was a great love of God and love of other people.'

We can give the last word to Jill herself, talking about the philosophy that drove her forward. 'I met somebody once who said: "I would never know you had been raped." What are we meant to do? Wear a sign? You have to carry on. And if that means that you look normal it doesn't mean to say that what's going on inside is anything that's normal.'

Scharlette Holdman

Born 11 December 1946; died 12 July 2017, aged seventy

Scharlette Holdman devoted her life to campaigning on behalf of death row prisoners in the USA. She even became friends with some of the country's most notorious killers. Her commitment to finding legal representation for them, and getting their sentences overturned, had a major impact on the US court system.

Scharlette was born in Memphis, Tennessee, which was then part of the segregated Deep South. For *Last Word*, Matthew Bannister spoke to David Von Drehle of *Time* magazine, who had interviewed Scharlette for his book on the culture of death row. He described first where the roots of her campaigning spirit sprang from: 'Her father was a landlord who owned property in the black part of town, [and] had impoverished tenants; when she was a high school student he used to take Scharlette with him when he went to collect the rents.' His aim seems to have been for Scharlette to learn the ropes of the family business. 'But what she actually took away from that were lessons having to do with the disparities of power, the oppressiveness of poverty. She came to identify very much with underdogs, and devoted her life to opposing authority.'

During the early 1970s, Scharlette was a civil rights campaigner. When the Supreme Court restored capital punishment in 1976 she began working in Florida, a state where death sentences were increasingly common. 'It was very personal,' says David Von Drehle. 'She got to know the men – mostly men – on death row. At first, she ran a little non-profit which was really just her and an assistant.' Discovering that most of the men on death row had nobody to represent them, 'she went around the state strong-arming, begging, pleading, wheedling lawyers to take these cases on pro bono. She would tell them that it wouldn't take that much time, that she would get them lots of help. And invariably these attorneys would end up years later, shaking their heads and rueing the day that they said yes to Scharlette.'

If at first it was all about getting these prisoners legal representation, it soon became more than that. 'The death penalty in the United States is a very complicated mechanism, where everything about the defendant has to be taken into account: their life stories, their background, the abuses they suffered, their mental capacity, on and on. So she created an art form called mitigation specialists – they referred to these as "mitigating circumstances".'

Scharlette would go to extraordinary lengths to prove mitigating circumstances, researching the defendants' backgrounds and hunting for evidence of mental incapacity. In one celebrated case the prosecution argued that the prisoner was mentally fit to be executed, because he had beaten the examining psychiatrist in a game of 'tic-tac-toe', or noughts and crosses. Scharlette described to the radio programme *This American Life* how she responded, drawing on her Southern roots to remember an exhibit at the Mid-South Fair where a chicken played tic-tac-toe: she wanted to find such a chicken and bring it into court. After all, as she put it with typical spirit, nobody would doubt a chicken: 'Chickens aren't going to lie, chickens have integrity.' The point was to show that being able to play tic-tac-toe did not equal an awareness of the consequences of your actions. Unfortunately, 'the court felt that bringing the chicken into the courtroom to play tic-tac-toe would degrade the dignity of the court. I thought that the dignity of the court was degraded by executing a mentally retarded, mentally ill person.'

Scharlette's campaigns brought her close to some of America's most notorious prisoners. David Von Drehle lists some of them: 'Ted Kaczynski, the Unabomber, became very fond of her; Eric Rudolph, the 1996 Atlanta Olympics bomber; Khalid Sheikh Mohammed, who was the accused mastermind of the 9/11 attacks ... she worked with all of them.' The obvious question is, did she have any qualms about working with people who were absolutely, no question about it, guilty of killing many people? David Von Drehle thinks not: 'I don't think she did have qualms. She felt that everyone deserved a fair trial.' His reading of Scharlette – that she was very much anti-authority – folded into this attitude. For her, 'there is no greater exercise of the power of authority than to execute someone, to take a life. And so she was determined to make that as difficult as possible for the state authorities.'

The work was the kind of crusade that can take over your whole life, and in Scharlette's case it did so. 'They really ran the whole operation on cigarettes and alcohol and coffee and nerves.' It was particularly difficult right at the beginning because she was then a single mum with two children. 'In one story her son came home from school and there was the family car with a big box in the back, and he said: "I hope that's not what I think it is?" And it was. It was a coffin with the remains of an executed inmate. His body hadn't been claimed, and so Scharlette had taken on the job of finding a place to bury it.'

As a person, her character belied the seriousness of her work. As Von Drehle says, 'You don't expect, when you are writing a book about the death penalty, to spend a lot of time laughing, but despite the work that she did, and the horrible stories, she managed to be one of the most charming and hilarious people I have ever met.'

How to quantify her impact on the American legal system? For Von Drehle, the answer is plain to see in the statistics: 'When she started her work, in an average year, something like 300 death sentences were handed out in American courts. That number has plunged to fewer than two dozen last year, and Scharlette is a big part of that.' She achieved this through the hard, attritional task of focusing on mitigation work. 'If she went out and talked to sixty people, a prosecutor would have to send someone out to talk to at least sixty people as well. And that's a very expensive proposition.' All of which made prosecutors think a lot harder about whether they wanted to bring a case to capital trial.

Sister Ruth Pfau

Born 9 September 1929; died 10 August 2017, aged eighty-seven

> *'If they really have to live such a life, then at least I want to share. I can't sit back and watch it. Sitting back and watching this is the worst, really, that can happen.'*
>
> Sister Ruth Pfau

Sister Ruth Pfau was a Roman Catholic nun who, after a childhood spent in Nazi Germany, became known as the 'Mother Teresa of Pakistan' for her work in combatting the spread of leprosy. The Nazis came to power when she was four, and the horrors she remembered of living though that time influenced her calling. After completing medical training she joined a religious order which sent her to India, via Pakistan. But a chance visit to a leper colony, and the appalling sights she saw there, meant she never left the country, instead dedicating her life to those most in need. The centre she established went on to treat more than 50,000 families, many of whom were horrifically disfigured by leprosy. Sister Pfau's efforts would see Pakistan become the first country in Asia to bring the disease under control.

Mervyn Lobo worked closely with Ruth and is now the CEO of the Marie Adelaide Leprosy Centre. He spoke to Kate Silverton for *Last Word*, recalling how Ruth's wartime experiences affected her: 'She would be very, very scared to stay alone in a room, especially a dark room, and she used to speak about her brother who died of hunger.' Ruth found herself, like many of her generation, asking what sense there was in life.

She came to Pakistan almost by mistake, says Mervyn Lobo: as a sister of a congregation called the Daughters of the Heart of Mary, she actually wanted to go to India, but visa issues mean that she was sent to Karachi in Pakistan. It was there that she first visited what was then known as a leper colony, in McLeod Road. 'When she saw the state of the lepers over there she was very much hurt.' She was a woman who had seen much suffering in her life due to the war, but, in her words, 'this drawn-out misery without any hope' was something else.

In Mervyn Lobo's description, at that time the lepers 'would be begging in the streets and being pushed around in a pushcart and you could see their eyeballs popping out, no nose, you could see the skeleton of a face and no limbs'.

When she first set out, she had only the most basic of resources. 'We started from a wooden hut, made of those wooden crates,' says Mervyn Lobo. 'She single-handedly went all over the country, and wherever she was getting patients, she would try to establish a centre.' That is where it began – she took on the work of funding the centres and training the staff. 'And this is how she spread this network that is now called the National Leprosy Control Program over 157 centres all over Pakistan.'

The number of patients being treated in those days was in the many, many thousands. 'MDT, the multi-drug therapy, was introduced somewhere in the early 1980s, and before that it was lifelong treatment.' Ruth herself explained that part of the struggle to establish this protocol was to convince people that the disease was treatable.

Ruth Pfau received numerous awards throughout her life, and she was awarded Pakistani citizenship in 1988. The fact that she was given a state funeral is a huge indication of how revered she was. 'She fully deserved this,' says Mervyn Lobo. 'Just imagine: a person who came in 1960, stayed all her life in Pakistan, who risked her life at times.' She had been willing to go into what were known as no-go areas, and dedicated her life to the cause. The result is that leprosy is under control, not only in Karachi but throughout Pakistan.

As to what drew her to Pakistan, Lobo points out that it was where her heart lay: 'Being a nun, she never wore her habit, she used to wear local Pakistani dresses, *shalwar kameez* – she was a beautiful lady. She always said: "I was born in Germany, but my heart's country is Pakistan."'

The last word here comes from Sister Ruth herself, explaining why she had dedicated her life in this way: 'I love the country.'

Davida Coady

Born 15 April 1938; died 3 May 2018, aged eighty

Davida Coady was an American doctor who travelled the world to help those suffering from hunger or in distress. From Biafra to India to Honduras, she worked tirelessly to save lives. Growing up in Berkeley, California, Davida was inspired to take up public service by a preacher at the local community church. She studied medicine at Columbia University. War erupted between Nigeria and the breakaway state of Biafra, leading to a massive famine during which 2 million people died; Davida joined the relief operation.

When Davida went there the country was in the wake of terrible starvation, and the military situation was precarious. Davida was asked to report back to the American government on what she had seen in Biafra, and, as her husband Tom Gorham recalls, she had to correct misleading accounts from others which played down the crisis: 'They were getting reports through the State Department that there was no famine, there were no bodies in the street, and the people there would look fat. She said: "Well, people get bloated when they are dying of starvation, and the Nigerian people bury their dead right away."' He points out that this illustrates one of Davida's main characteristics: 'She wasn't afraid to challenge the powers that be.'

A few years later, Davida travelled to India as part of the team trying to eradicate smallpox. She described her love for India and Bangladesh, forged from her travels as she went around in her Land Rover, often following dirt roads to remote villages. 'I love to look now at pictures of Indians and see that nobody under thirty has got smallpox scars. That just chokes me up.'

This was not a person who needed the creature comforts. Her husband laughs as he recalls her telling stories of 'riding on elephants bareback, and four-wheel drives across swamps'. He describes how, in spite of her appalling phobia about snakes, he has pictures of her wading through Central American swamps. 'She was a very determined individual, let me tell you. Nothing was going to get in the way of helping her fellow man or woman.' Not even snakes.

This determination was again on display in November 1981, when she went to Honduras to help refugees from the civil war in El Salvador. They were crossing the border in the aftermath of an incident when a special battalion of the El Salvadoran Army, trained by the USA, had systematically massacred hundreds of people including women and children in one day and night.

Davida's friend Sarah Shannon worked alongside her there: 'We could be in the middle of *chaos*, but when she was talking with somebody, or assessing a patient, or assessing a situation, she would just get incredibly focused and her judgement was always quite rapid, and usually extremely accurate.' The other side of her job was to meet with officials, whether that meant the United Nations representatives or the Honduran military. 'She would argue really forcefully about what needed to be done, and she would argue very articulately, making medical arguments to back it up, fiercely defending what she thought was right.'

Once she was back in the USA, she dedicated her time to helping people closer to home. In particular, she was focused on addiction and drug abuse. As she herself put it: 'The biggest cause of homelessness, and crime, and misery, and violence, and child abuse, in my community is substance abuse.' This was eventually to lead to a new chapter in her personal life when she came home from working in the developing world. As her husband Tom describes it, she 'kind of reinvented her life. She wanted to work with poor alcoholics and addicts . . . I am a formerly homeless person, I was on the streets for over ten years, a hopeless alcoholic. She, being an admitted alcoholic herself, wanted to be of service to those of us, like me, who were living on the streets, in jails.' Tom was in fact in a cell when they met. Not that it was love at first sight on both their parts: he used to 'tease her, and call her a quack with a ponytail, and she'd fire back at me and pick on my Irish and stuff. I wondered what the heck she was doing messing around with people like me.'

Sarah Shannon gives one clue to what lay at the heart of Davida's determination: 'Over the last few months of her life, as I was helping her correct her memoir, I noticed that she actually didn't mention any of the many awards that she had won over the course of her life. And she said: "Well, those aren't important, what's important is the work and that the work gets done."'

And, when questioned on whether or not she derived a sense of satisfaction from knowing that she had helped such a large number of people, her husband is emphatic. 'You know, she had to. You would never hear it from her, but she had to have had a huge sense of accomplishment.'

Jan Ruff O'Herne

Born 18 January 1923; died 19 August 2019, aged ninety-six

For fifty years Jan Ruff O'Herne kept secret the ordeal she'd suffered during the Second World War. But in 1992 she finally revealed that she had been forced to work in a brothel for Japanese officers, where she was repeatedly raped. She went on to become an outspoken campaigner against the use of rape as a weapon of war.

Jan's story began when she was born, in 1923, into a Dutch colonial family in what was then the Dutch East Indies and is now Indonesia. By her own account, 'I had the most wonderful childhood.' Her daughter, Carol, speaking to *Last Word*, explained that from a young age her mother had a vocation: 'She was a very devout Catholic and she was hoping to become a nun,' though of course it is hard to tell what fate would have prescribed for her had the war not happened. As it was, fate intervened in 1942. She was staying with friends in the resort owned by her French grandfather, Henri, up in the hills. 'That's where the Japanese came, up that hill, and that's where they were ... taken as prisoners.' In Jan's own words, 'When the war in the Pacific started and then the Japanese invaded Java in March 1942, that is when all the beautiful life finished.'

She and her family were taken to a prisoner of war camp, where for two and a half years they lived in appalling conditions. 'It was terribly difficult in that camp. Women and children were dying all the time and they had nothing to eat.' Jan set about trying to keep people's spirits up, establishing a 'little makeshift school' and looking after children, which was something she loved – she had 'a magic touch' with children. But even this came to an end when the Japanese officers called out all the young girls in the camp. She was among the unlucky ones chosen. They were 'forced into a truck, with all the mothers and everyone crying, and ... someone pushed a handkerchief into her hand'. The girls were taken to a house where 'they were given rooms and flowers were put in vases next to the beds, and they were all given different names, Japanese names of Japanese flowers'. It was at night time that the Japanese officers arrived.

Jan herself later described in matter of fact terms what happened next: 'There stood this large, fat, bald Japanese officer looking at me, grinning at me.' She fought him to no avail, telling him she would not do it, 'and he said, "Well I will kill you. If you don't give yourself to me, I will kill you." And he actually got out his sword. I never thought suffering could be that terrible. I was in total shock.' This ordeal was repeated, hundreds of times, over a period of three months.

The handkerchief that she had been given as she was driven away from the camp became a curious artefact when, one day in a period of quiet before the officers returned, she was sitting with the other girls, 'and she pulled out the handkerchief and she put it on the table and in the middle she wrote her own name and the date, and she asked all the girls to sign their names'. She had some embroidery thread, and she resolved to embroider all their signatures on to the handkerchief. It is, says her daughter, a piece of 'tangible physical evidence', something that she would later donate to the Australian War Memorial Museum where it is on display.

As the war drew to a close the Japanese transferred the women to a camp, swearing them to secrecy about what had happened in the brothel on pain of death. They were eventually liberated by British troops. When the war ended a priest visited the camp, and, mindful of her earlier vocation, she told him her story and said: 'Father, I want to be a nun but this is what's happened to me, I've been raped hundreds of times.' His answer? 'My child, under the circumstances, after what's happened to you, you can't become a nun.' It is an attitude that continues to shock her daughter: 'I've always thought, what? Why would you still be a Catholic after that?' But Jan rose above it.

Among the troops who liberated the camp was a British soldier called Tom Ruff. As soon as he and Jan started a relationship, she told him about her history. He said, 'I still love you and I don't hold it against you and I'm going to tell my commanding officer.' He made that report, but nothing was ever done about it. Jan also told her mother, but her mother advised her never to speak about it again, because it was so upsetting.

There were physical after-effects to her ordeal. She found it hard to get pregnant and had repeated miscarriages, which a doctor told her were a result of the damage her body had sustained. Psychologically, though, her daughter marvels at her resilience: 'The amazing thing about my mother is that she didn't seem to have any psychological after-effects . . . and that's why when she finally spoke out everyone said, "Oh no, not your mother!"'

In 1992 she was prompted to go public about her ordeal by another conflict halfway round the world, when she saw that women were being raped in the Bosnian conflict. 'Then I saw on television the Korean comfort women . . . the first ones to speak out . . . They wanted justice and compensation and an apology more than anything else.' But they weren't getting what they wanted. Seeing this Jan thought, with typical bravery, 'I must back up these women. Now is the time to speak.'

Her daughter feels that it was not so much speaking out that healed her mother's wounds. But she used her pain 'to do something really positive. She used it for the good of women like her, she used it for the good of women in the world, and in the world to come, and women from all countries.' It became her mission. In Carol's view, that last part of her life 'was in a way her greatest passage', because of how she turned her pain into something positive.

Jan thought of her own story as 'a message of faith and forgiveness'. She wanted to ensure that such a thing would never happen again, her words encapsulating the fortitude and compassion with which she lived her life: 'That is why I tell these stories, I never want any other women to suffer as I did.'

Abebech Gobena

Born 20 October 1935; died 4 July 2021, aged eighty-five

Abebech Gobena was sometimes called the Mother Teresa of Africa. She devoted her life to helping the poor children of her native Ethiopia. The organisation she founded, Agohelma, initially looked after orphans but then expanded to offer healthcare and education to hundreds and thousands of disadvantaged youngsters. Abebech was employed as a quality control inspector with a company that exported grain and coffee when she was inspired to start her humanitarian work.

Elias Mulugeta Hordofa was a colleague of Abebech before becoming a BBC journalist in Addis Ababa. He talked to *Last Word* about her challenging early life: at aged ten she was married against her will to a man who was older than her. 'But she didn't accept that from the start and eventually she ran away from that marriage and fled to the capital, Addis Ababa.' She managed to survive, and even to marry again when she was ready.

She would tell the story of how she had become involved with caring for children. It happened when she went on a pilgrimage to the north, where there was at the time a famine. 'She saw lots of starved people lying around all over the place,' and one particularly shocking incident was to prompt her into action. Her own description of this moment is harrowing: 'I came across a woman who was breastfeeding an infant and I tried to feed her, but she did not respond. I was very shocked and started shaking her, thinking I could wake her up, but she was dead.' According to Elias, she felt unable to abandon that child, so 'she took her and she hid her and brought her back to Addis Ababa'. And then she adopted another child, and that was how it got started.

Those first two children were one thing, but she kept adding more and more, and by the end of the first year she had taken in about twenty-one. 'That's when it started causing problems,' says Elias. Not only her husband but also her mother began to object, 'questioning her, her mind, her sanity. They gave her an ultimatum.' In fact, her husband asked her to choose between the children and him. She chose the children. This meant leaving him, and 'they started from scratch in a little shelter'.

It seems extraordinary that she went from that tiny shelter to finding the funding to grow her institution. She managed it by sheer determination, and by being as inventive as possible. They would sell vegetables at the side of the road, and later make jewellery and other objects to trade, 'and eventually she managed to get registered, make the organisation legal,' and even get some government help.

It grew enormously, eventually comprising a school and a hospital. Its fundraising activities included a printing press and the capacity to sell spices and other foodstuffs. Part of the aim was to help train the children as they grew so they could start their own businesses. The reaction to Abebech's death was overwhelming: 'The whole country was very sad, even the prime minister said they were heartbroken.' But they were thankful, also, for her enormous contribution to the country.

Remarkable Lives

It can feel as though every entry in the *Last Word* archives is the starting point to a terrific movie. In this section, the background settings are rich ones – the Beat movement; the beautiful wilds of Exmoor; the golden age of Hollywood – and the central characters compelling. The stories vary hugely in scope: some are small, almost domestic scenes; others are sweeping sagas.

One of the many pleasures of listening to *Last Word* is the way that some lives cast a focused beam on the age in which they were lived. Here we find unexpected sidelights on familiar subjects – how extraordinary to meet a woman whose life felt the reverberations of a century's worth of conflict, or who was part of one of India's most powerful and tragic dynasties. How moving to meet a concentration camp survivor whose subsequent life defied the horrors she saw there. This section celebrates those who were witnesses to history: women with whose deaths we lose not only a remarkable character, but a link to the past.

Olga Kevelos

Born 6 November 1923; died 28 October 2009, aged eighty-five

Olga Kevelos had an eventful life: she worked on barges during the Second Word War, became an international motocross champion, retired to run a pub, and took part in the TV quiz Mastermind. *Olga grew up in the Birmingham suburb of Edgbaston. She had an academic bent, studying metallurgy and developing an interest in astronomy. After the war she went to Paris to study French medieval history, but it was her wartime experiences and her motorcycling exploits that fascinated the regulars at the Three Tuns in King's Sutton, which she ran with her brother Ray.*

One of Olga's friends, and a member of her pub quiz team in the village, was David Bridson. He told Matthew Bannister of *Last Word* that Olga was part of a group known as the 'Idle Women' during the war. 'The "Idle Women" were the volunteer women who manned the barges on the Grand Union Canal primarily during the war.' It was around 1943 when they put out advertisements for women to work on the barges. 'Olga answered an ad in *The Times* at some point in 1943, because she was desperately bored by the office work that she was doing at that time.' Olga's own description of the job gives not only a vivid sense of what it involved, but also of her lively way of speaking: 'You tied the boat tight into the chute, then they wound up the shutters and all of a sudden, you had about thirty tonne of nutty slack, come bang! down into the hold.' They then had to 'trim' it, or level it out, shovelling it so that the boat was balanced. While it was clearly hard work, it was also 'a kind of freedom that some of us might never have known until we had got married'.

Far from being for 'idle women', it was an arduous job, explains David Bridson: 'It was the born-and-bred canal people that referred to them as idle women.' The name derived from the IW badge they wore on their lapel – standing in fact for Inland Waterways, but reimagined by the canal people. 'According to Olga they worked anything from eighteen to twenty hours per day, in very rough living conditions, and always very hungry. Unlike the land girls, for example, they didn't get extra rations; they had to make do with what everybody else got, so she told me that she was always hungry at that time.' Tough though it was, and hungry though she was, Olga enjoyed the work – she revelled in the camaraderie and in later years remembered the 'nice bits', the summer days when they sat and played their recorders.

She got involved in motorcycling through one of her boyfriends, said David Bridson. He was a keen motorcycle racer, and 'I think she was keen to see more of him at the weekends, so she decided to borrow a big bike.' She went on to take part in motocross, and especially in the Six-Day Trials both in Scotland and in international competitions (the International Six-Day Trials are the oldest and some of the toughest off-road competitions in motorcycling). She won two gold medals, something that she was very proud of, according to David. 'Generally people don't recall just how tough those Six-Day Trials were. The famously macho Steve McQueen was himself an entry in the International Six-Day Trials in 1964.' He was described as being up against the toughest riders in the world, and this was in the year that Olga was riding.

Olga had a wicked sense of humour, and was very much the kind of person you would want on your side in a pub quiz team. She was, David says, 'extremely knowledgeable; she had her specialisms of course and she had her weaknesses. Her weaknesses tended to be things like soap operas, and pop music, and celebrities ... Her strengths were primarily science and geography, and history.' And Genghis Khan, which was the subject she chose on *Mastermind*.

She did so many varied things and had so many different aspects of her life. David Bridson speculated that the key to her spirit and curiosity came originally from her family. 'She had a very interesting family: her father was a Greek financier, her family came from the Mani, which is a part of Greece which is famous for its fighting spirit. And, I suppose, she evinced that spirit.'

She remains the only woman to have won two gold medals at the International Six-Day Trials.

Hope Bourne

Born 1920; died 22 August 2010, aged ninety

Hope Bourne was a self-styled champion of Exmoor, a woman who for more than two decades lived alone in a tiny caravan in the middle of the wilderness. Hope wrote several books about the history of Exmoor, its animals, plants and rural traditions. From 1970 until the early 1990s she lived off the land, shooting animals, growing vegetables and claiming to survive on an income of just £1 a day, half of which she saved.

Hope Bourne was the subject of two documentaries, the second of which, in 1981, was made by Gerry Dawson. He tracked down the famously reclusive Lady of Exmoor by writing to Hope Bourne, c/o Withypool Post Office, Somerset. He spoke to Matthew Bannister for *Last Word*, describing that first encounter: she had written back to him to say she would meet him at Landacre Bridge. This was a place in the middle of Exmoor 'which I knew was far away from where her own home was. It was as if, like a wild animal, she was protecting her lair.' He duly turned up at the bridge at ten o'clock on a Tuesday morning. 'When I was waiting on the bridge, I saw a very small, stooped figure moving through the gorse and I knew it was Hope, and after a while she came down to meet me.'

That documentary yielded some beautiful recordings of Hope, her rather lilting voice explaining what drew her to live the way she did: 'To live in the midst of this lovely landscape and be able to do the things I like doing, and to walk out and see all its beauty and refresh myself with it and have the perfect freedom to go anywhere I wish, at any time that suits me – that is in itself riches.'

Gerry's description of what Hope looked like conjures some of the rigours of her life: 'She was a very small woman. If you see pictures of her from the 1960s or 1970s, you'd see her pick up a bale of hay, and she was little taller than that hay bale stood on end, she was tiny. But she could carry that hay bale.' By the time she met him, she had been living in the wilderness for nearly twenty years; she had originally started this way of life in around 1963, says Gerry Dawson, and around ten years later had moved into 'a very dilapidated fourteen-foot caravan' in the early 1970s, By the time of the documentary, 'the caravan was in a terrible condition, it was falling apart and held together by baler twine; it looked like it could blow away at any time'.

The joy that Hope got from the landscape sings out from her words, her soft, almost whistling, accent capturing the beauty of the place she loved so much: 'When you get the odd fine day it is so lovely because the clarity of the light and the freshness of the atmosphere, the blue of the sky, the light, the gliding clouds and sunlight on the hills is *so* beautiful that you can forgive the climate all the rest of its unpleasantness . . . And you get this sense of primeval wilderness, it has the effect of being infinite.'

As to what drove her to take part in the documentaries, it was the cause of the wilderness itself. She was a fiercely private woman, says Gerry Dawson, who didn't want fame, but who did have one motivation: 'The one thing that she wanted to talk about, most importantly, was that the wilderness quality of Exmoor was being threatened by constant tourist development. The appearance of information boards and signposts and pathways everywhere – in opening the wilderness to tourists it was taking away the very wilderness quality that she thought was important for everybody.'

He describes her as 'like an Edwardian lady, very well read,' in spite of a lack of formal schooling. 'She wrote books which are a delight, she lived on nearly nothing: she hunted her food, she grew some vegetables, she fed off rabbits and fish, and maybe the occasional deer.'

That 50p a week she saved 'accounted for cartridges for the gun, because the gun was very important for the pot, matches for the stove, and paraffin for the stove, and if, rarely, there was any little left over there was one weakness she definitely had. She seldom had it, but she loved chocolate, she was an addict for chocolate.'

But though she lived entirely immersed in nature, she wasn't entirely cut off from wider events going on in the towns and cities: 'When the Countryside Alliance were campaigning about hunting, it was Hope Bourne that went to Downing Street, although she was then very old.' To her, it was a cause worth fighting for, so she was willing to make the trip. And as she herself put it: 'It is a great mistake that some people seem to think that I must be some sort of a recluse, because I live in a place like this. I most certainly see lots of people and have lots of friends.'

Even her own name seems evocative, as Gerry Dawson points out: 'It couldn't be more beautiful, could it really? It expresses the inexpressible.' If you are in Exmoor and look inside the churches there, you are likely to find a trace of Hope, 'because you are virtually certain to find a little picture done by Hope, just signed: Hope L. Bourne'.

It seems right to give such a spirited woman the last word, her light, clear voice setting out the philosophy that lay at the heart of her unusual life: 'If I cannot be a leader, at least I will never be a follower. And if God has not willed that I should not be a master in life, at least I will never be a servant.'

Shirley Verrett

Born 31 May 1931; died 5 November 2010, aged seventy-nine

Shirley Verrett was an African-American soprano who overcame racial prejudice to become an international opera star. Her career took off in the 1960s, with performances in the role of Carmen at the Bolshoi Theatre, the New York City opera and La Scala. She went on to sing both mezzo and soprano roles at many of the world's leading opera houses.

Professor Christopher Brooks helped Shirley to write her autobiography, and he talked to Matthew Bannister for Last Word *about what it was that first made him a fan: 'I guess I was still in high school at the time. She did a recital, in Baltimore, Maryland, and I was just riveted to the intensity of her singing.' According to Professor Brooks, Shirley's parents were not in favour of her being an opera singer: 'Not at all. They came from a Seventh-Day Adventist background, so she actually began singing very early, as a result of her hearing her mother.'*

Shirley herself talked of how early she began to sing, with her mother discovering her voice when she was only five and a half. 'She must have heard me humming or singing around the house, some tune or hymn that I heard in church. And she said: "I want to teach you a little hymn."' Her mother taught her the hymn, and when she sang it to her father, who was himself musical and had learned about the technical aspects of breath control, 'I was five and-a half years old and he started telling me about the diaphragm.'

It isn't surprising to hear from Christopher Brooks that she faced racial prejudice right from the outset of her career: 'Of course, American society was very segregated. African-Americans knew their place, they knew how far they could go, or where they could live and those kinds of things.' What that really meant for her was brought home when she moved to New York and the conductor Leopold Stokowski invited her to sing with the Houston Symphony Orchestra. 'And the Houston Symphony Board, when they found out that she was African-American, rejected her; and the maestro called her [and said] in a very clear and committed voice: "You *will* sing with me."' He made good on his promise, and the following year when he was conducting the Philadelphia Orchestra he invited her to sing with them. 'That was one of those defining moments, because she got to be on the stage with a major orchestra, at the time, in a solo role, and that would lead to several other opportunities taking place.'

Without doubt, Christopher says, her favourite role was Bellini's Norma. 'She could identify with Norma as a mother, and she could identify with Norma being a good friend, as Norma is to Adalgisa.'

Shirley was particularly popular in Italy, where they called her 'La Nera Callas', the black Callas. This stemmed from her performance in *Samson et Dalila* at La Scala. 'Her feeling was that, where Italians were concerned with opera, "You could be black, white, or green, or purple, but if you sing well, they will love you."' And they did.

Astrid Aghajanian

Born 28 March 1913; died 10 June 2012, aged ninety-nine

Astrid Aghajanian was a witness to seismic events in world history. As she herself put it, in an interview recorded by the Imperial War Museum, she was caught up in four separate wars. In each war, she lost her home, and each time she had to start over with nothing.

Astrid's tribulations began at a very early age. She was born into an Armenian family in Elbistan, Southern Turkey, in 1913. While she was still a baby she was caught up in the wholesale massacre of thousands of Armenian people under the Ottoman Empire, as her daughter Sophie recalled for *Last Word*: 'My mother's father had been conscripted into labour battalions which started in 1915.' The Armenian men were not armed, but they were conscripted for work purposes, and, 'after the job was done, they would be killed. So it was a way of getting rid of the men.' And so it proved, as Astrid's account illustrates in spare but shocking detail: 'My father came and kissed me and told my mother: "I know that they are going to shoot me." And they took him, and they shot him.'

Sophie takes up the family history: 'My grandmother talked about being in a horse and cart with my mother and being taken to the Deir ez-Zor desert, which they had already heard was like a killing field.' Survival relied on her being as ingenious as possible, and when her mother found herself, alone with Astrid, surrounded by dead bodies and with the Turks intent on killing as many Armenians as they could, she hid them both among the bodies, so that the Turks thought they had killed everyone. 'They collected their horses and they went,' Astrid put it simply. The next day, her mother picked her up, and they set off into the desert barefoot.

There they met a Bedouin. Sophie tells how he gestured at her grandmother 'and told her to go with him'. Not knowing the language, she refused by indicating in sign language. At which point he sold both mother and child, and put Astrid's mother to work waiting on his two wives. She was willing to do anything to save her daughter and get to Aleppo.

Eventually they did reach Aleppo and were reunited with Astrid's uncle. Her mother married an Armenian man who was serving in the British Army, and they were posted to Palestine. In 1942 Astrid married Gaspar Aghajanian and she became a teacher, settling in Tiberias. However, as the struggle to establish the state of Israel became violent, once again the family lost everything. After a time as refugees Astrid's husband was granted British citizenship and they settled in Cyprus.

Sophie describes how 'they finally made a very nice home for themselves. But of course in 1974 the Turks invaded, and they were living in the North.' Once more the family were at the mercy of forces beyond their control. Astrid's mother was still alive. 'She had managed from other relatives to salvage one or two things like a little patchwork Bible in Armenian, and so on, from her past.' She had also saved a wedding photograph, which she gave to Astrid as a last memento of her father. But, like everything else, it was looted when the Turks invaded and Astrid and her husband once again had to flee. 'They went to the British base and then were flown to England.'

By now in her sixties, Astrid and her husband had to start all over again. They settled in Shoreham-by-Sea in West Sussex. She was widowed in 2007. From her daughter's description of her character we sense a spirit that held on to a love for life no matter what was thrown at her: 'She was very outgoing, actually, she loved people, she was a great cook and believed in the medicinal properties of food and herbs, but of course all this she'd learned from her mother, who was a very resourceful woman, who was very capable.' She took pride in her appearance and was always 'very elegant . . . she embraced life'. Everything she did she wanted to do well.

Astrid lost a lot through the conflicts she had been through in the course of her life. But she became determined that the trials she had been through would not make her bitter. 'When one goes through all these atrocities one can be either fierce, vicious, or can be very kind and polite.' Astrid's choice was to embrace her humanity, and choose kindness: 'I don't like to hurt anyone. And when somebody hurts others, I hate it.'

Carolyn Cassady

Born 28 April 1923; died 20 September 2013, aged ninety

The writer and artist Carolyn Cassady was an important figure in America's Beat Generation. She was married to Neal Cassady, had an affair with Jack Kerouac, and vied for her husband's affections with Allen Ginsberg. In Kerouac's seminal 1957 novel On the Road, *Cassady was portrayed as Dean Moriarty and Carolyn was Camille, his long-suffering wife.*

Carolyn came from an unlikely background for an icon of the counterculture: she was born into a middle-class family and went to an exclusive all-female college in Vermont. It was while she was studying theatre design in Denver, Colorado that she first met the charismatic, but serially unfaithful, Neal Cassady. At the time he was married to his first wife LuAnne – named Marylou in *On the Road* – but nonetheless he made a pass at Carolyn. At their first meeting, Neal 'didn't talk much, he just looked, and his looks were rather laser-like'.

Their son, John, spoke to Matthew Bannister for *Last Word* and picked up the story from there. 'What happened was some girl she knew had a spare room in the city, in San Francisco, and so she moved out there because it was closer to Hollywood than Denver, and Neal followed her. And so Kerouac followed him and then Ginsberg followed him.' They spent their time in jazz clubs, 'and they would go to these jazz clubs every night, you know, with Carolyn and they just loved it, this whole scene'.

In some ways she kicked off the whole West Coast counterculture: 'She was the catalyst,' says John. 'I would tease her: "Yeah Mom, it's all your fault." And she goes: "I am not taking responsibility for hippies and the anti-war movement," and she denied the whole thing. But I said: "Well, you trace it back, you were the germ, with Neal, and Jack and Allen following him out there.'"

Kerouac continued to be involved in their lives: 'Jack lived in our attic when he wrote a lot of *On the Road*,' says John. Carolyn described Jack as 'very self-absorbed, but very romantic . . . and very good-looking'. The domestic set-up was unconventional.: 'I had two husbands at the same time.' Or as John Cassady elaborates: 'Jack was living with us. Neal had to go to work one night; at the door he turned around and gave them a wink and said: "My best pal and my best gal," because they were mutually attracted to each other too. But he kind of condoned it, and so Carolyn went along with it because she didn't want to lose Neal. In other words, it was a twisted scene.'

Allen Ginsberg was also very much in love with Neal, and Carolyn caught them in bed together: 'She comes home, and Neal is in the middle, LuAnne [Cassady's first wife] is on one side, and Ginsberg is on the other, in bed . . . She wasn't pleased,' adds John drily.

In Carolyn's own words: 'We both loved the same man, I just felt sorry for Allen that I had what he wanted.' But in spite of all these complications, Carolyn remained very much in love with Neal, and in John's words, 'put up with him for fifteen, twenty years'.

In *On the Road* Carolyn's alter ego Camille was the symbol of all that was stable: it was she who brought some sense of steadiness to this rackety lifestyle. 'Carolyn had respect, she was a lady.' In Jack's novels, the Neal character repeatedly lets her down.

Certainly Carolyn was tested to the limit when Neal's infidelities also involved hoodwinking her so that he could blow their life savings on a horse. According to John, 'He was seeing . . . a little redhead, really cute, but crazy: that's how he liked them! So, one day, [Carolyn] gets a phone call from the Bank of America and they say: "Mrs Cassady, I am really sorry, but we forgot to have you sign this one form." And she goes: "What?" And they say: "When you were here this morning withdrawing your money." She went: "Uh-oh!" And she said: "Tell me something, do I have red hair?"

And the guy goes – he is on the phone, right, he can't see her – and he goes: "What?" She asks: "Do I have red hair?" And he goes: "Yeah." So then she knew exactly what happened.' Neal had taken his girlfriend to the bank and she had signed Carolyn's name.

It turned out that Neal had withdrawn 10,000 dollars, bet it on a horse after a tip, and lost it. Unsurprisingly, Carolyn 'freaked'. But according to Carolyn, no matter how much she suffered she never lost her love for him.

John agrees that it was in part in response to other people telling the story of her life that Carolyn eventually wrote her own book, *Off the Road*, which was published in 1990: 'I think it was a large part of it, because people would just make stuff up.' She had written an enormous volume after Neal's death in 1969. Excerpts, especially the bits involving Neal and Jack, were published under the title *Heart Beat*. But there was more to Carolyn than just her relationship with Neal. She was an artist, with a life beyond the Beat scene.

Heart Beat was also the title of a movie in 1980, with Sissy Spacek as Carolyn and Nick Nolte as Neal. The memory of this makes John Cassady laugh: 'It was horrible; it was the worst movie. We were on the set for almost the whole shoot and Sissy and Nick couldn't try harder, but the script was horrible.' However, Carolyn never intended to be defined by the Beat Generation. As she put it herself: 'We never, ever, thought of it as any sort of movement, or generational thing or anything like that.' Jack, she said, was 'trapped into it'.

After Neal's death, Carolyn moved to the United Kingdom and ended up in a mobile home in Bracknell, Berkshire. It seems likely that the people in Bracknell never had any idea of the past life of the woman living among them: 'She just didn't make any friends, you know, she was kind of private, and she just didn't go over to the neighbours with an apple pie ... She just pretty much kept to herself. I don't think anybody even knew who she was.'

Luise Rainer

Born 12 January 1910; died 30 December 2014, aged 104

Luise Rainer was a double Oscar-winning actress whose Hollywood career ended when she fell out with the mogul Louis B. Mayer. Luise was born in Germany in 1910, to a wealthy family. Her father objected to her making a career as an actress, but she persevered nonetheless. As a teenager she impressed the great director Max Reinhardt, who cast her in plays by Pirandello and Shakespeare. Then, as her daughter Francesca Bowyer recalled for Matthew Bannister on Last Word, *she was spotted by a talent scout from the Hollywood studio MGM: 'He was supposed to scout for another actress, went to the theatre, saw my mother, and sent a message to Louis B. Mayer: "Stop everything, you have got to see this actress. She is amazing!"'*

Luise's own account gives a sense of the slight remove she felt from Hollywood: 'When they called me to come to Hollywood, I thought: well, this is all mad. I was on the stage with Reinhardt, I was part of a wonderful group . . . I only made one single condition, it was that I was permitted to bring my dog with me.' Hollywood had not been her aim: 'I didn't feel like I was a beauty or anything like that, I didn't care about the money I made, it didn't matter to me. And all those standards, which were standards of Hollywood, were not my standards, and, somehow, I felt I didn't fit in.'

The scene that made her name came in the 1936 film *The Great Ziegfeld*. It is known as the 'telephone scene' – Luise had the part of Ziegfeld's French first wife, Anna, and it takes place when she hears that he has found someone else. Francesca Bowyer explains what it was in that scene that so touched the audiences: 'The pain of finding that her husband was married . . . and the joy of hearing his voice, and the remarkability of her being able to combine both emotions, in one, was quite extraordinary.' It was that which won her the Oscar.

Twelve months later, in 1937, she became the first person to win two Oscars in consecutive years, this time for her performance as a Chinese peasant woman in *The Good Earth*. As for her attitude to these honours, Francesca tells a revealing story: 'She was very flippant about her Oscars.' One of them, which had been used as a doorstop, was getting somewhat the worse for wear. When Francesca asked if she could have it, Luise's response was to call the Academy and say '"I need another Oscar" and, only in Luise Rainer fashion, they presented her with a new Oscar!' She had ended up with 'two good Oscars and one which was the leaning tower of Pisa. And I said: "Mummy, what happened with that one Oscar that you wouldn't let me have?" And she said: "Oh darling, the electrician came, I didn't have enough cash to give him, so I gave him the Oscar." There is some electrician, in Nugano, who has an Oscar, and probably doesn't know what it is!'

Francesca's account of how Luise's Hollywood career came to an end is not so light-hearted, but nonetheless gives a sense of her strength of character. It came when she was married to Clifford Odets, the playwright, and she was wrung out by this difficult marriage. 'She had done one film after the other, and she walked into Louis B. Mayer's office and said, "L.B., I need a vacation, I need to find my soul." And he said, "What do you need a soul for, you've got a director, don't you?"' He asked her to sit on his lap. Her answer was, '"I don't sit on anybody's lap." And he said, "Well, all the other stars do." And she says, "Well, not me. I'm leaving on vacation." He said, "You leave now, and you will never work in this town again. We made you and we will break you." She said, "Mr Mayer, I am now in my twenties. When I am forty, you will be dead, and I will still be alive, because God made me, you didn't." And she walked out.'

It was the mark of a resolute character. 'She was always very strong, very wilful, she was wonderfully manipulative with all her charm, and she could charm the birds out of the trees.'

She certainly charmed some extraordinary people. She had contact with Albert Einstein and with Bertolt Brecht. In fact, she brought Brecht over to America to get him out of danger during the war. Nevertheless, this exchange with Sue Lawley, from the *Desert Island Discs* she recorded in 1999, gives a wonderful sense of Luise's personality:

'Brecht wrote a play for me, called *The Caucasian Circle of Chalk*, and it was actually I who gave him the idea for it.'

'But you never played it?'

'No.'

'Why not?'

'I didn't want to work with Brecht.'

'Why not?'

'I didn't like him.'

She came back to acting later in life because she loved it. As a mother, her daughter describes her as 'the eye of the storm, and you never knew whether to have your umbrella up or not. Maybe it would have been better if I was a boy. But she did love me: we did have some *wonderful* times . . .' Francesca tells a fitting anecdote: 'I remember sitting with her in a restaurant not three years ago, and we were sitting next to a few young women on a banquette and they said, "What do you attribute your longevity to?" And she said, "I had a terrible life." And I looked at her and I said: "Mummy, exactly what about your life was so terrible?" I said, "You were born to fortune, you became an overnight star; you married a man who you were madly in love with; you married my father, who was a saint; dare I say you had me. You knew only people that we read about in books; you travelled all over the world, you lived at the best addresses, what exactly was so terrible about your life?" So she gives me this ethereal look, up to the heavens, and never answered.'

For the last words on Luise Rainer, perhaps it is best to turn back again to her *Desert Island Discs* interview. When asked what her luxury would be, her words are simple:

'My luxury – you can't give me that.'
'What is it?'
'To be missed, by the many people I love.'

Lotte Hass

Born 6 November 1928; died 14 January 2015, aged eighty-six

In the 1950s, Hans and Lotte Hass made undersea films which delighted television audiences. On expeditions to the Red Sea, the Caribbean and the Great Barrier Reef in Australia, the couple brought the rich variety of underwater life to the screen.

Lotte Hass was described in the press as 'one of the most beautiful women who has ever prowled under the sea with a spear'. She was nineteen when she first met Hans Hass, who was already a well-known underwater explorer, as Reg Vallintine of the Historical Diving Society explains. 'She was lying sunbathing at the swimming pool, with a friend, and the friend said: "I have heard that Hans Hass is looking for a secretary, are you interested?" She said: "No, no, no, I have my place booked for university, but I would like to meet him." He disappeared, this friend did, and came back and said: "He will see you in half an hour!" No time to change, she had this interview, and he said: "Can you do shorthand?" And she said: "No, but I can learn quickly," and she thought: I would love to get on one of these expeditions.' Or as she put it herself later on: 'Why should not women explore under the sea, as they do on land? We can swim, and we can dive as well as men can.'

To convince Hans to take her on the expedition, 'The first thing she did was to learn breath-hold diving at the local swimming pool.' When he continued to refuse her, she 'borrowed his camera and leaped into the Danube in the middle of winter, nearly froze to death, but took some wonderful photos of fish, including a giant pike'. That got her photos into the papers. His comment then was: '"Not bad: what a pity you are not a man!"'

Nevertheless, she joined his expedition, accompanying him first of all to Port Sudan and then to the ruined city of Suakin. Hans hired a pearl diver's dhow, and Lotte 'had to sleep on the deck with the crew and the expedition members and several thousand cockroaches and a million flies'. The land was incredibly barren, and incredibly hot. But as Reg Vallintine explains, 'She survived all that. The cameraman who had come out from Austria wilted in the heat at once and begged to be allowed to go back, which he did on the next plane. And so she said: "Well you are an expedition member short, I'm your girl!" So Hass said: "Oh, well, all right," and then pronounced: "Well, from today you are a man."'

And so she set off to do the filming. It was considered to be highly dangerous to dive in the Red Sea at the time, or in the Caribbean – we know now that this isn't true, but that was the perception. 'Hass was pursuing sharks, chiefly, manta rays, these huge rays. Lotte quickly learned to use the oxygen breathing apparatus that they were using, and she was pretty fearless.'

Lotte was blonde and petite, and made a huge impact on the viewers in the 1950s. She had a tremendous effect, says Reg: 'Half the young men in Britain were in love with Lotte Hass.'

But she was more than just a pin-up. The films made by Lotte and Hans Hass were mould-breaking at the time. People hadn't seen beneath the ocean in this way before: 'Nobody had swum underwater with large animals and that was dramatic, and exciting.' As a woman, she inspired many to take up the sport: 'When the British Sub-Aqua Club was formed in the early 1950s, it meant that more women straight away came in slowly to a male-dominated sport, because of Lotte Hass.'

Shobha Nehru

Born 5 December 1908; died 25 April 2017, aged 108

Shobha Nehru was a Hungarian-Jewish woman who married into India's most influential political dynasty. Her husband was B. K. (Braj Kumar) Nehru, former ambassador to the USA and cousin of India's first prime minister. Shobha was also very close to Mahatma Gandhi.

She was born Magdolna Friedman in Hungary, but as persecution of Jews spread through Europe her parents changed their names to Forbath, so at school Magdolna was nicknamed 'Fori', which stuck for the rest of her life. Her great age meant that she could remember events of the early twentieth century, including the outbreak of the First World War, according to her daughter-in-law Chanda Nehru. She had been six years old, and clearly recalled sitting on a train in the station when her father picked up a newspaper and said, 'War has been declared.' By the time she was twenty, strict quotas were in force for Jewish students at Hungarian universities, so her parents sent her to the London School of Economics. It was here that she met and fell in love with B. K. Nehru. After overcoming her parents' opposition, the couple were married, and Magdolna became Shobha Nehru. She threw herself into her new Indian identity, according to Helen Barry, the South Asia Bureau chief of the New York Times: *'Before she travelled to India, she did two things: one is that she learned Hindi, and the second is that she got off the ship when she arrived in a sari, and decided that this was going to be her life, her complete life.'*

Shobha was taken around the country to meet her husband's relatives, and one of the meetings was with his cousin Jawaharlal, who was then in prison. By her own account, she 'fell in love with the way he was', and was distraught and in tears when the jailers came to take him away. He was allowed to write one letter per month, according to Helen Barry, and his next letter was to her. 'The thrust of the letter was: if you are going to be part of this family, you should know that Nehrus don't cry in public.'

The seismic shock that was about to hit her adopted country was of course Partition. Her reaction, typical of her compassionate nature, was to try to help refugees. Helen Barry describes that time: 'Muslim families were gathering in just huge numbers in an old fortress, and they were fed, and housed, and protected from the mobs outside, and they were being put on trains up through Punjab into Pakistan. And Fori Nehru, she would pack these families, the children and the grandparents ... on to trains, night after night, and she said that one night she found that everyone on the train had been dragged off and killed.'

She also opened a small shop to allow refugees to sell craft work so they could make a living. This enterprise grew and grew and sixty years later is a huge government concern called Cottage Industries Emporium. Partition was followed, in 1948, by the assassination of Mahatma Gandhi. This was an event to which Shobha was a close witness, telling her daughter-in-law later that she was on the scene so soon after he was shot that she saw his body on the ground.

By 1966 her cousin by marriage (and Jawaharlal's daughter), Indira Gandhi, had become India's third prime minister. Helen Barry says that Shobha 'was very close, and very affectionate, with Indira'. She stayed off the subject of politics, with one exception: 'In the 1970s Indira Gandhi declared a state of emergency in which many civil liberties and freedoms were rolled back, and one of the most atrocious elements of this period was a campaign of sterilisation.' So many people approached her with personal stories of this atrocity that it moved Shobha to remonstrate with Indira directly, saying, 'Indu, look, you know I never talk to you about politics, never, no. *Please* look at this.'

In 1984 Indira Gandhi herself was assassinated, and once again Shobha Nehru was a witness, the emotion breaking through in her voice as she recalled it later: 'She was in the dining room laid down on the ground, I was sitting next to her, but she wasn't there, that was the end of it too.' Helen Barry emphasises the recurring nature of tragedy in Shobha's family: 'The life, as part of that family, was one characterised by blow after blow after blow. Gandhi was assassinated, Indira was assassinated, and then Rajiv was assassinated, and it was a family that then had to live with this chronic sense of siege.'

Through it all, she kept her mischievous side, says her daughter-in-law: when she was ninety-eight a young couple came to visit her with their child, 'and the mother introduced herself and said: "Here is my son, mother," and the father stepped in and said: "Well, I am the father." So she stopped for a moment and she looked up and she said: "Well, fatherhood is always a matter of conjecture!"'

Daisy Kadibil

Born 1923; died 30 March 2018, aged ninety-five

Daisy Kadibil was the youngest of three girls who walked 1,200 miles across Australia in the 1930s after being taken from their parents by the government. Daisy, who was eight at the time, her older sister Molly and their cousin Gracie found their way back to their home town of Jigalong by following the rabbit-proof fence which ran for large distances across the countryside. Their story became a bestselling book and then a successful film. The girls had white fathers and Aboriginal mothers and were victims of the government's policy of separating mixed-race children from their families, with the eventual aim of eradicating the Aboriginal race.

Christine Olsen wrote the screenplay for and co-produced the film *Rabbit-Proof Fence*, and met the sisters for her research. 'Molly was a very stern sort of woman, strict in a way, whereas Daisy was much more relaxed. She was the one ... who gave me most information about the walk back ... the one who told the story. She had a very beautiful, wide, serene, sort of face and she laughed a lot.'

Molly and Daisy were the children of Thomas Craig, who worked as an inspector on the rabbit-proof fence, and a woman from the semi-nomadic Martu Aboriginal people. As Christine Olsen describes, this put the girls right in the firing line of the policies of the government: 'The Western Australian government were taking away part-Aboriginal children and putting them into institutions. Eugenics was in lots of people's minds: they really felt that the Aboriginal race was going to die out.' There was a sense that the children should be taken out of the 'primitive' world and taught 'right' from 'wrong'.

As Christine Olsen described it, 'Mr Neville, who was the chief protector of Aborigines in Western Australia, heard about these girls and arranged for the policemen to go and get them. They were picked up from their extremely remote home in Jigalong, and taken to a place outside of Perth. And Molly, the oldest, took one look at the place and said, "We're going, I don't like this at all."'

So they started walking. 'They either stole food or they were given food by homesteaders, who would then ring Mr Neville to tell him that they had just fed these girls.' They walked for about 1,600 kilometres, more than halfway across the continent – 'a *huge* achievement'. The girls were pursued by police and trackers, but after walking for two and a half months finally made it back to Jigalong.

The girls eventually married, but they hadn't entirely escaped from the traumatic policies of the government. In later years, Christine Olsen says: 'Molly had two children, and her little child was taken by Mr Neville a few years later and she never, ever, saw her again.' Daisy stayed in Jigalong. She married and worked as a cook.

She also describes Daisy's reaction to the film. It came out in 2002, and the world premiere was in Jigalong itself. 'Daisy had no idea of what was going on: she didn't know what a film was. She had no idea that this would go around the world and her story would touch people, because of course everyone fell in love with Daisy, the littlest one.'

'I think that it was very easy to have an intellectual understanding of that stolen generation and how the government had removed children and taken them away. But I think what *Rabbit-Proof Fence* did was to make people aware emotionally of what it actually means to have your child taken away from you.' Daisy's story – part of a shameful chapter of Australia's history – was heard around the world.

Gena Turgel

Born 1 February 1923; died 7 June 2018, aged ninety-five

Gena Turgel was a concentration camp survivor who married the British soldier who liberated her. She was one of the first to tell the distressing story of the camps in public, and wrote a book about that time called I Light a Candle. *Throughout her life Gena worked with educational groups to make sure the Holocaust was not forgotten. In 1985, on the fortieth anniversary of the liberation of the camp at Bergen-Belsen, Gina went back there with her husband Norman. Also on the trip was the journalist Paul Martin, who described for* Last Word *his first impressions of the couple: 'I noticed this very elegant-looking lady, very well dressed, very polite, very sweet-looking, and her husband; they seemed to be very close, literally holding hands.' It turned out that not only had they been at the camp when it was liberated, but they both had extraordinary stories.*

Karen Pollock, chief executive of the Holocaust Educational Trust, knew Gena well. She spoke to Matthew Bannister for *Last Word* and started by outlining the bare facts of Gena's life: 'Gena was born in Krakow, she was one of nine siblings. She was sixteen when the Nazis occupied Poland, and she ended up in the ghetto.' While there, she witnessed one sibling being killed, and heard of the death or disappearance of some of the others.

She, her mother and two of her sisters were sent to the Krakow-Plaszow concentration camp. Gena would later describe the fate of one of her sisters, who had been working in Schindler's factory: she was kidnapped on the way to her quarters and was taken to hospital to be experimented on. Gena tried to see her, but it was forbidden.

Gena was one of those who was then force-marched to Auschwitz, and then to Buchenwald. Many of the people on that march died en route. The others reached Belsen. In Gena's own words: 'Eventually, the train stopped, and they opened – I can still hear today, I'll never forget – the locks, how they were, the noise.' The Germans called Belsen an extermination camp, or *Vernichtungslager*. 'From there is no escape. And I just could not believe my eyes. Walking skeletons in every sense of the word.'

After that, says Paul Martin, she spent a couple of years in the camp. 'But fortunately for her she was in the infirmary and was dealing with ill people, mainly of course those who were privileged to be serving as officers, or as Nazis, not the camp inhabitants themselves. She did in fact treat Anne Frank, just as she was dying of typhus.'

In 1945 her life was to change. Karen Pollock describes what happened: 'She saw from her window and heard an announcement that the British had arrived.' And among those British troops was Norman Turgel. According to Paul Martin, 'Norman Turgel had actually been one of the very few people who drove up in a Land Rover to the front of that camp *before* the British forces had got to that part of Germany.' He 'took a shine' to Gena, says Karen Pollock; or, as Gena herself said: 'He made up his mind when he first saw me in the hospital, in that white overall, that this – I – was the girl that he was going to marry.'

According to Karen Pollock, he asked if she would have dinner with him and took her to the officers' mess. 'She walked in and there were beautiful white tablecloths and flowers on the tables.' It must have been an extraordinary moment for somebody who had been in the camps. But the next moment was even more surprising: 'He said: "This is your engagement party."'

Gena's reaction? 'She said: "What are you talking about?" But the long and short of it is, he had decided that he wanted to marry her.' Their wedding, officiated by the British Army chaplain there, was the first one to take place at the camp. 'Her dress was made out of a parachute.'

They came to live in the UK, and had a very happy marriage: 'A wonderful, long-lasting marriage. She was a mother, grandmother, great-grandmother. It was a huge family.' To listen to Gena Turgel describing her husband is to restore faith in fairy-tale endings: 'He was a wonderful, wonderful, man. He was my everything, my lover, my friend, my liberator, my husband.'

As Karen Pollock says: 'I smile when I think of her. She had a wry sense of humour, she was determined and resilient, and she felt very strongly that she was spared to be a voice for the voiceless.' She went on using that voice for the rest of her life: 'I am thankful to God that I am here, able to tell that story to people who haven't got a clue what went on. And younger generations and generations to come should never, never, experience what I have experienced.'

Sources

Eileen Nearne
'They put me in a cold bath ...' from Personal File Eileen Nearne HS9/1089/4, National Archives
'I was arrested ...' ibid.
'I did not want to work ...' ibid.

Alix D'Unienville
'They were real professionals ...' from Alix D'Unienville's own account, quoted in Marcus Binney: *The Women Who Lived for Danger, The Women Agents of SOE in the Second World War*, Hodder and Stoughton, 2002, pp. 288-90
'In thinking of it ...' ibid.
'Many of my comrades ...' ibid.

Jeannie Rousseau
'Have fair fallen, O fair ...' from 'Henry Purcell' by Gerald Manley Hopkins: *Gerald Manley Hopkins: Selected Poetry*, Oxford University Press, 1996, p. 128.

Asma Jahangir
'Mostly I have heard people say that there is a glass ceiling through which you have to go ...' from *Taking a Stand*, Episode 1, Series 2, BBC Radio 4, 01/01/2002
'We didn't see ourselves as gender specific ...' ibid.
'She [the woman] came into my office and said: "My parents are here, and they are here to murder me."' ibid.
'This was a challenge ...' from 'The Life and Loves of Asma Jahangir', *Outlook*, BBC Radio 4, 12/02/2018
'Now, even the very right-wing religious parties ...' ibid.

'There have been times I have been scared . . .' ibid.

Daphne Park
'In the Congo you could get hit on the head at any time . . .' Source unknown
'You can't be a good one unless you trust . . . .' ibid.
'That was more risky for him than for me in a way . . .' ibid.

Lolita Lebron
'It was my idea and our idea, all of our idea.' Source unknown

Cristiane Desroches Noblecourt
'We can't save it! . . . It is finished, we leave it' . . . Source unknown
'I thought – *Philae* has not been moved . . .' ibid.

Dekha Ibrahim Abdi
'people from differences . . .' Source unknown
'*all* groups around the world . . .' ibid.

Nusrat Bhutto
'I have been followed here today . . .' *Tonight*, BBC One, 05/02/1979
'Military coups d'etat never last long . . .' ibid.

Fiona Gore, Countess of Arran
'when the village policeman wasn't looking . . .' Source unknown
'the sheer boredom of sitting at home and doing nothing . . .' ibid.

Beryl Platt, Baroness Platt of Whittle
'I was writing flight reports . . .' *Woman's Hour*, BBC Radio 4, 27/04/1983
'We really thought we were helping . . .' ibid.

Mary Ellis
'Everybody was flabbergasted . . .' from *Spitfire Women*, Love Productions, 18/09/2010
'You could go up and play with the clouds . . .' ibid.

Margaret Rule
'and Percy Ackland, who I always called our underwater gun dog . . .'
from *The Reunion*, 'The Mary Rose'. BBC Radio 4, 29/08/2004
'We were working eleven feet beneath . . .' ibid.
'Leather shoes, seamen's combs . . .' From *Outlook*, BBC World
Service, 01/02/1979
'Initially there was no way, legally, of protecting the *Mary Rose* . . .'
from *The Reunion*
'That is absolutely ludicrous . . .' ibid.
'We have worked night and day . . .' ibid.
'If I had left her there, a) I would have had a much less worried
twenty years . . .' ibid.

Jo Cox
'She was someone who had a heart of gold . . .' Source unknown
'Nobody was singled out for her . . .' ibid.
'Batley and Spen is a gathering of typically independent, no-
nonsense towns and villages . . .' From Jo Cox maiden speech,
Hansard, House of Commons Deb 03/06/2015, Vol. 596, Col.
675, Devolution and Growth across Britain - Hansard - UK
Parliament
'I'm proud that I was made in Yorkshire . . .' ibid.
'She were a people person, she were for us . . .' Source unknown

Beatrice de Cardi
'I wouldn't hesitate to pull my dress up if I had to slide down a bank
. . .' Source unknown
'I found innumerable sites that other archaeologists had just passed
by . . . . . .' ibid.
'I don't think I resemble Indiana Jones in many ways . . .' ibid.

Aline Griffith, Countess of Romanones
'Everybody seemed to be working on one side or the other . . .'
Source unknown
'Sitting at a table in front of a small electronic box . . .' from *The Spy
Wore Red*, Aline Griffiths, Blackstone Audiobooks, 2000

'He leaned down to a lower drawer, and pulled out a metal container' ibid.

'In her undercover days ...' from *Sisterhood of Spies: The Women of the OSS*, Elizabeth McIntosh, Naval Institute Press, 2009

Alex Timpson

'They went from me to a children's home.' From *Lowri*, 'Fostering', BBC Two 29/9/1998

'I remember my mother coming to me and saying ...' ibid.

Anne Coates

'I was at boarding school ...' from *Front Row*, BBC Radio 4, 07/12/2016

'David said, 'Well it's nearly perfect ...' ibid.

Hilary Lister

'It is freedom, it is me alive ...' from *Hilary Lister's Round Britain Dream*, BBC Two, 14/07/2013

'The boat is where I am me ...' ibid.

Marita Lorenz

'they said we don't like his uniform, we don't like his beard ...' Geraldo Rivera Interviews Marita Lorenz, 1991, Geraldo Rivera - Part 2 - Marita Lorenz - YouTube

'He said, "Oh who gives a shit, who is going to prove it?"' *Timewatch*, BBC Two, 07/10/1992

Wangari Maathai

'And so I thought: why not plant a tree? ...' Source unknown

'It's one of the most beautiful creations ...' ibid.

Elinor Ostrom

'We now have over 200 forests that we have studied around the world ...' Source unknown

'What we have ignored is what citizens can do ...' ibid.

Rita Levi Montalcini
'[I] continued to work, completely ignoring what was happening around me' Source unknown

'like finding oneself on top of the highest peak ...' from Rita Levi-Montalcini – Banquet speech. 6/12/2022. NobelPrize.org. Nobel Prize Outreach AB 2022 https://www.nobelprize.org/prizes/medicine/1986/levi-montalcini/speech/

The Rev. Joyce Bennett
'and that was when he began to play at being the vicar ...' Source unknown

'In a private capacity, amongst friends, ...' ibid.

Janet Rowley
'I was a physician, my husband was going to Oxford ...' Source unknown

'I think science should be exciting ...' ibid.

Billie Fleming:
'You don't. You can't tell the difference ...' from Billie Fleming interview with David Barter, *Cycling Weekly*, 6/5/2014

'I liked it.' ibid

'After having ridden for only two weeks ...' from Billie Fleming's diary

Stephanie Kwolek
'What I love about my work is that I have the opportunity to be creative every day ...' Source unknown

Lorna Wing
'You can't treat autism ...' From 'A World of Their Own', *Horizon*, BBC 2, 14/1/1984

Jerrie Mock
'I looked down at the houses and the little tiny cars ...' Source unknown

Claudia Alexander
' OK, I cried . . .' Source unknown

Valerie Hunter Gordon
'It seemed extraordinary . . .' from *The One Show*, BBC One, 02/6/2015
'I ended up making over 600 . . .' ibid.
'Everyone wanted to stop washing nappies . . .' ibid.

Margaret Pereira
'We have a lot of old clothing . . .' from *Woman's Hour*, BBC Radio 4 , 01/09/1982
'On that occasion I was able to show . . .' From *Forensic Detection*, BBC Radio 4, 21/08/1970

Maryam Mirzakhani
'My main interest is understanding structures you can put on a surface . . .' Source unknown

Diane Leather
this 'barrier that was waiting to be broken . . .' Source unknown

Jan Morris:
'faintly romantic . . . the surgeon was a very dashing elegant young Frenchman and there was music in the street outside . . .' *Woman's Hour*, BBC Radio 4, 29/03/2003
'It wasn't just the normal sort of marriage of love and sex, it was also a marriage of friendship . . .*Desert Island Discs*, BBC Radio 4, 16/06/2002
'I believe very much in the continuity of life, and I don't believe in death really . . . '*Profile*, BBC Radio 4, 01/06/ 1978

Nicki Chapman
'My parents were told that I wouldn't live more than eight hours . . .' Source unknown
'I think they obviously worried . . .' ibid.

'I can't tell you the number of times I have sat . . .' ibid.

Patricia Stephens Due

'We had been foot soldiers . . .' Source unknown

'So what you did was important . . .' Source unknown

'They come in, and we are not used to them sitting down beside us . . .' Source unknown

Mabel Cooper

'I think this story is to tell people that it is wrong to shut people with learning difficulties away.' From *BBC Breakfast*, BBC

'They called us hurtful names like idiots, and moral defectives . . .' ibid.

'When you're eleven and you go into these big buildings . . .' ibid.

'. . . very frightening. Very frightening when you come out of a hospital . . .' ibid.

'People outside, they don't understand . . .' ibid.

Helen Bamber

'I felt as the war began to draw to an end that I would have to go to Germany . . .' Source unknown

'My most vivid memory of Belsen, and Germany, was of people who would grab hold of you . . .' ibid.

'I would be worried if we were no longer distressed . . .' Source unknown

Efua Dorkenoo

'I had to deal with a woman with the most extensive FGM . . .' from Women of the World (WOW) Festival 2014 on FGM, Southbank Centre, https://southbankcentre.co.uk/blog/female-genital-mutilation.

Debbie Purdy

'He was told to be nice to me . . .' From *Woman's Hour*, BBC Radio 4, 07/08/2009

'I had been told that . . .' ibid.

'If somebody needs counselling . . .' ibid.
'It is really difficult . . .' ibid.

Jeanne Córdova

'very much in love with God and Mary and all that . . .' Source
    unknown
'I remember seeing organised women sitting around.' Source
    unknown

June Jolly

'You see, I approached it from such a different point of view . . .'
    Source unknown
'Even after I had been in charge I still had to fight theatres, anaes-
    thetists, surgeons, matrons . . .' ibid.

Ruth Gruber

'I have two tools to fight injustice . . .' from *A Jewish Heroine: Ruth
    Gruber*, Shalom TV, 18/10/2011
'Somebody has to go and hold their hand . . .' ibid
'At one point, three Nazi planes flew over us . . .' ibid.
'These strong young men were defiant . . .' ibid.
'I think the truth can make us free . . .' ibid.

Jill Saward

'I want people to understand . . .' from *Everyman*, 'No Great
    Trauma', Touch Productions, BBC One, 16/09/1990
'You have to bury it and bury it dead' . . . ibid.
'I met somebody once who said . . .' ibid.

Scharlette Holdman

'Chickens aren't going to lie . . .' from '*This American Life*, Poultry
    Slam 2011', Episode 452, 02/12/2011

Sister Ruth Pfau

'If they really have to live such a life, then at least I want to share
    . . .' Source unknown

'I love the country.' ibid.

Davida Coady
'I love to look now at pictures of Indians ...' Source unknown
'The biggest cause of homelessness, and crime, and misery, and violence, and child abuse ...' Source unknown

Jan Ruff O'Herne
'When the war in the Pacific started ...' from *Australian Story, Australian Comfort Woman Jan Ruff-O'Herne*', ABC News, ABC, 2001
'There stood this large, fat, bald ...' ibid.
'Then I saw on the television ...' ibid.
'That is why I tell these stories ...' ibid.

Olga Kevelos
'You tied the boat tight into the chute ...' Source unknown

Hope Bourne
'To live in the middle of this lovely landscape ...' From *Hope Bourne on Exmoor*, HTV, 1997
'When you get the odd fine day it is so lovely ...' ibid.
'If I cannot be a leader ...' ibid.

Shirley Verrett
'She must have heard me humming or singing around the house, some tune or hymn that I heard in church ...' Source unknown

Astrid Aghajanian
'My father came and kissed me ...' from *Interview*, Imperial War Museum Catalogue no 17368, 19/03/1997
'They collected their horses and went ...' ibid.
'When one goes through all these atrocities ...' ibid.

Carolyn Cassady
'very self-absorbed, but very romantic ......' Source unknown

'We both loved the same man . . .' ibid.
'We never, ever, thought of it as any sort of movement, or generational thing or anything like that . . .' ibid.

Luise Rainer
'When they called me to come to Hollywood . . .' from *Desert Island Discs,* BBC Radio 4, 28/03/1999
'Brecht wrote a play for me . . .' ibid.
'My luxury – you can't give me that . . .' ibid.

Lotte Hass
'Why should not women explore under the sea, as they do on land? . . .' Source unknown

Shobha Nehru
'. . . fell in love with the way he was . . .' from '*A journey of Thoughts with Fori Nehru*', Doordarshan National, www.youtube.com/watch?v=IxExHVqp2lw&t=2600s, 2011
'Indu, look, you know I never talk about politics . . .' ibid.
'She was in the dining room . . .' ibid.

Gena Turgel
'Eventually, the train stopped, and they opened . . .' *Remembrance Week,* Episode 1, Series 3, BBC One, 05/11/2012
'He made up his mind when he first saw me . . .' ibid.
'He was a wonderful, wonderful man . . .' ibid.
'I am thankful to God that I am here . . .' *Holocaust Memorial Day, A Survivor's Admiration for British Troops,* Forces TV, 28/1/2014

All efforts have been made to trace original sources. If any have been unintentionally omitted or misattributed, we invite copyright holders to contact us so that any errors can be corrected in future editions.